FOOTPRINTS ON THE SANDS OF TIME

A History of Worstead

For the people of Worstead

The lives of great men all remind us
We can make our lives sublime,
And, departing, leave behind us
Footprints on the sands of time.

Henry Wadsworth Longfellow (1807-92)

FOOTPRINTS ON THE SANDS OF TIME

A History of Worstead

Written by **Peter Brice**

Designed and illustrated by **Stefan Ganther**

Assisted by **Rosemary Rix** and **Ron Barrett**

ISBN 978-0-9932813-0-3

First Published 2015 by Worstead Parish Council

© Worstead Parish Council

This publication is available direct from Worstead Parish Council

<u>*www.worsteadpc.norfolkparishes.gov.uk*</u>

<u>*clerk.worsteadpc@gmail.com*</u>

Printed by Barnwell Print Ltd, Dunkirk, Aylsham, Norfolk
www.barnwellprint.co.uk

The unavoidable CO2 generated from making this paper has been reduced to net zero through the purchase of carbon offset credits in the Andipatti wind project in India. The project reduces CO2 emissions by displacing electricity which would have otherwise been drawn primarily from fossil fuel power stations. The project has also contributed to the local economy and livelihood of residents through job creation.

Cover photo – One of the graffiti footprints from the ringing chamber in St Mary's tower, by Stefan Ganther

Inside cover – One of the Green Men of St Mary's and the Worstead Heritage Trail logo – Drawn by Stefan Ganther

CONTENTS

PREFACE

4. GEORGIAN WORSTEAD

5. VICTORIAN AND EDWARDIAN WORSTEAD

6. WORSTEAD IN THE TWENTIETH CENTURY

7. WORSTEAD IN WHITE COTTAGE

8. THE FUTURE OF WORSTEAD'S PAST

Fig 1 Worstead Aerial View 1946
Courtesy Norfolk County Council NHER NAPL-RAF collection ref. TG32/TG3026/AMeri

PREFACE

The parish of Worstead lies in north Norfolk in the Tunstead Hundred and in the Waxham Deanery. The parish now covers some 26,000 acres of slightly undulating land, most of it good farmland. To the north-east its boundary is the River Ant, formerly the Smale. A small tributary of the Ant forms Worstead's southern boundary. To the west and north the parish boundaries lack clear physical definition. Neighbouring Westwick may have been a part of the Saxon settlement of Worstead: the place-name element *wic* means *settlement* or *farm* but the <u>west</u> wic would make more sense if it were part of Worstead. So Westwick's clear western boundary in Westwick Beck may once have been Worstead's boundary. To the north a more indefinite boundary line runs through the former heath that separates Worstead and North Walsham.

Worstead has four main claims to fame. First, it gave its name to the cloth called worsted, and for some six centuries the weaving of worsted was as vital to the economy of Norfolk as it was to that of the parish. Second, the profits from worsted cloth rebuilt the Church of St Mary the Virgin, a cathedral-size 'wool' church, with an outstanding Perpendicular exterior that is in Norfolk's top ten. Third, Meeting House Hill, formerly Orpley, took its modern name from the Baptist settlement founded there in 1717: the group of buildings clustered round the rebuilt Chapel of 1829 is unique among the remains of nineteenth century Nonconformity. And fourth, the North Walsham and Dilham Canal, was built in 1825-26 from Antingham Ponds to Dilham, giving Worstead access to the River Bure near Wayford Bridge from the staithes at Briggate and Meeting Hill. The canal straightened the winding River Ant. Unusually it never had a towpath for draught horses, because it was largely used by sailing wherries, although there was a 'hailing' path so that men could haul the boats if need be. Yet there is much more: Worstead has a rich agricultural history; a wealth of fine listed buildings; an interesting educational heritage; and a community that both provided the church and has since ensured its survival, not least through the Worstead Festival, which celebrates its golden jubilee in 2015.

The aim of this study is to set Worstead in its Norfolk context through time. Chapter 1 starts with a brief survey of Worstead's prehistory and moves on to Worstead's entries in the *Little Domesday Book*, which is where Worstead's written history begins. Chapters 2 to 6 are broadly chronological with several recurring themes running through them: the manufacture of worsted cloth; farming; religion, with particular reference to the churches and chapels; the schools; the built environment; the relief of poverty; commerce and communications. Certain important episodes find their rightful place in the chronology, notably the Great Plague or Black Death of 1349 and the English Rising or Peasants' Revolt of 1381. Chapter 7 - 'Worstead in White Cottage' - is an attempt to show what light the story of one property can cast on the wider history of the parish in the hope that other folk might wish to explore Worstead's past through the microcosm of their own dwelling. Chapter 8 seeks to outline the responsibility that we all have to secure the future of Worstead's past.

Fig 2 View from St Mary's Tower c1950s (author unknown)

This study is the culmination of a long process. It sets down what I have learned about Worstead's history since 1999. I was spurred on by Douglas Harding, who urged me to make use of the papers he had collected on Worstead; by Catherine Wilkins, formerly Worstead's District Councillor, who shared her researches with me; by Gavin Paterson, himself a fount of knowledge about the Worstead he loves: and by the many Worstead folk who have shared their stories and local knowledge with me. However the most creative spur was the Lottery-funded Spinning a Yarn in Worstead Project, the brain-child of the late Brian Morgan, chairman of the Worstead Guild of Weavers, Spinners and Dyers. It led to a partnership of the Guild, the Parish Council and the Parochial Church Council to promote Worstead's heritage. Four of us, Stefan Ganther (the designer and coordinator of the Spinning a Yarn Project), Ron Barrett (for the Parish Council), Rosemary Rix and I planned the Worstead Heritage Maps and Trails, which were unveiled by Norman Lamb MP at the Worstead Festival in July 2012. The four of us thank Dr Mike McEwen for his fine drawings on the Trail Maps and Leaflets; Father Anthony Long for his wholehearted support for the siting of the Heritage Maps in the churchyard and for his wide knowledge of St Mary's; Jean Crome for giving us entry to hidden parts of St Mary's; Laurie Ashton for allowing access to the amazing undercroft of St Andrew's Cottage and for drawing attention to many details in Worstead's buildings; and the Parish Council and especially Johanna Gardner, its Clerk, for supporting the Heritage Trails and for publishing the fuller guide to them on the Parish Council's website. All four of us are endebted to the Norfolk Historic Environment Record and to the Norfolk Record Office.

In this text italic numbers in brackets refer readers to the Trail Maps in St Mary's churchyard, to the brief Trail Leaflets (available in St Mary's or in the White Lady public house), and to the fuller text that can be found on the Parish Council's website or by googling 'Worstead Heritage Trails.' References are also made to the Norfolk Historic Environment Record (NHER followed by a number) which can also be found on-line.

At succeeding Festivals and on other occasions Stefan and I have led many guided tours of the village centre: they have added a good deal to our knowledge because many participants have asked searching questions and have pointed out things that we had not noticed! Stefan and I owe especial gratitude to Ron Barrett and Rosemary Rix. Ron initially proposed a blue plaque scheme to publicise Worstead's fine architecture and history, but chose to abandon it in favour of the Heritage Maps and Trails, for which he worked so hard behind the scenes. Rosemary Rix shared with us both her sources and her wide knowledge of Meeting Hill and its relationship to the wider parish. She eased our way through the bureaucracy of the Church of England and offered many creative suggestions to improve the text. We are also extremely grateful to Sharron Ganther for the proof-reading that has saved us from many errors.

I have been responsible for writing the text, and Stefan for all matters relating to design and illustration. He also shares in the ownership of the text in that he has been my constant foil: he has made me (and everyone within earshot!) look at buildings with fresh eyes; he has found sources, maps and illustrations; he has required me to justify my conclusions; and he has suggested many improvements, not least the pattern which the text has followed. I have tried to do justice to the historians whose works are listed in the bibliography: if a date appears in brackets after an author's name in the text, his or her publication is detailed in the bibliography. There is, of course, no such thing as a definitive history, because new evidence comes to light and successive generations of historians ask new questions of the old evidence. So what I have written is necessarily provisional: the wealth of history in the parish of Worstead merits further research, as chapter 8 suggests. I have done my best to read the historical sources accurately and to eliminate errors, but any mistakes that may appear are my own. Please tell me where you know I have gone wrong.

I owe some more personal debts of gratitude: to the late Brian Morgan for asking me to speak at the Weavers' *Built on Wool* event in 2010; to Ian Rendall for his encouragement and for much information, not least in *Worstead Woven* (2000); to Brian Hedge and to Neil Storey for their many photographs, both published and unpublished; to Chris Birks for his discussion of the archaeology below the former Market Place; to Nicholas Groves for his advice on many aspects of church history; to Des Hooker for his loan of Victorian books and magazines; and to the late Betty Marples who gave me her collection of programmes of the Worstead Festival. I owe most to my wife Margaret for her constant encouragement.

Peter Brice   May 2015

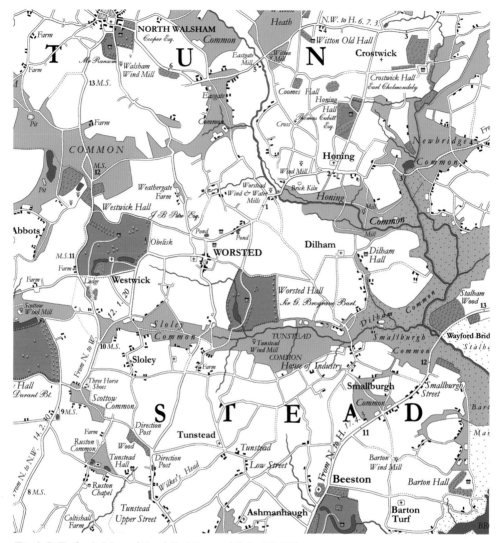

Fig 3 © Faden's Map of Norfolk (First published 1797)
Digitally redrawn by Andrew Mcnair 2006.

1. DOMESDAY WORSTEAD

1. Worstead's prehistory

Prehistory is usually defined as the period before history can be written from documentary sources. So Worstead's prehistory lasts until the eve of the Norman Conquest, because few records in East Anglia survived the Danish invasion of 866-70 and the periods of Danish rule thereafter. The earliest written reference to Worstead may date from 1046 when it was listed as one of the holdings of the Abbey of St Benet at Holme in a charter of King Edward the Confessor, but the charter is probably spurious. Worstead's three entries in the *Little Domesday Book* provide two brief snapshots of Worstead, one just before 1066 and the other in 1086, and the written history of Worstead begins with them. Most of what we know of the parish before 1066 comes from studying its geology, archaeology, place-names and topography.

Worstead's loamy soils are laid over sand and till. The glaciated stones, quite frequently found, indicate that much of the landscape was formed in the Ice Ages, when ice-sheets and glaciers advanced south in the cold glaciations and receded in the warmer interglacial periods. At the height of the Anglian glaciation of c.470,000-420,000 BC, ice covered almost all of East Anglia. At the end of the Devensian glaciation of 75,000-13,000 BC you could walk from Norfolk to Denmark, but global warming after 8000 BC caused sea levels to rise, flooding what archaeologists have called 'Doggerland' and creating the North Sea. Underlying Norfolk are layers of chalk which contain flint. Flint, often combined with brick and more rarely with limestone, is the lasting building material of late medieval and early modern Worstead (timber, wattle and daub, and clay lump were frequent but impermanent materials). Two types of fossil are relatively common in the parish: echinoids (sea urchins) and belemnites (squids) show that the sedimentary rock below Worstead is relatively young in geological terms, belonging to the Jurassic period (c.200-142m years BP - Before the Present) or the Cretaceous (c.142-65m years BP).

From time to time Worstead's fields, gardens and ditches give up minor archaeological finds: prehistoric worked flints, including the occasional scraper; Bronze Age pot boilers; oyster shells, probably medieval, usually found close to dwellings; some unglazed pottery, probably no earlier than medieval; much more glazed pottery, relatively modern; knapped facing flints lost out of the medieval flushwork of the Churches of St Mary and St Andrew, sometimes with lime mortar still adhering; animal teeth and bones, some of them unbutchered; hand-made window glass; bottle glass, mostly quite modern; iron work related to farming and rural trades, much of it blacksmith-made but still fairly modern; and an early modern coin or two. Together they testify to considerable activity in the parish, some of it before Worstead's written history began, but most of it post-medieval.

More significant archaeological finds made in the parish are detailed in the Norfolk Historic Environment Record: two Neolithic polished flint axeheads (NHER 7573, 17513); a Bronze Age stone axe-hammer (NHER 11398); a decorated unlooped Bronze Age palstave axe (NHER 11132); a ring ditch (NHER 49221) which appeared as a cropmark on an aerial photograph in 1976 and probably marked a Bronze Age round barrow; an Iron Age gulley or ditch now beneath Jasmine House between Front and Back Streets (NHER 41157); but - as yet - no evidence from the Roman period, although a Roman road ran through nearby Sloley and Roman finds have been made across the valley of the River Ant in Dilham. The finds from Worstead suggest some pre-Roman activity in the parish but probably little permanent settlement, because the landscape was then quite wooded.

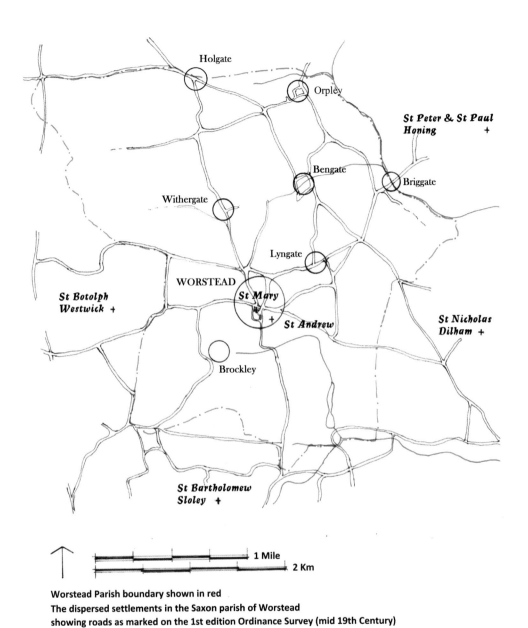

Worstead Parish boundary shown in red
The dispersed settlements in the Saxon parish of Worstead
showing roads as marked on the 1st edition Ordinance Survey (mid 19th Century)

Fig 4 Worstead Parish Map showing roads and dispersed settlements c1066.

Evidence for settlement before the Norman Conquest comes from place-names. The name *Worstead* is Saxon and means *the site* (*worth-*) of an *enclosure* (*-stead*), though it came to mean *farmstead* or *homestead*. So

Worstead probably means *the site of an enclosed farmstead or homestead.* The *-stead* ending may also indicate that Worstead began as a farm cut out of woodland or waste. Five of Worstead's seven outlying hamlets end in *-gate* which in Danish or Old Norse means *street.* This ending suggests that the five hamlets were named in the late ninth or early tenth century, but they may have had an earlier Anglo-Saxon existence. *Bengate* means the *street through the bean field*; *Briggate* the *street over the bridge*; *Holgate* (near the Recycling Centre) the *street through the hollow*; *Lyngate* the *street though the flax field* (or possibly *lime trees*); and *Withergate the street through the willows* (a Nicholas *de Salicibus - from the Willows* - is recorded in Worstead in 1334-5). The names of the other two hamlets have Saxon derivations: *Brockley* (around Worstead Station) means the *badger's clearing in the wood* and *Orpley* (now Meeting Hill) *Orp's* (or *Eorp's*) *clearing in the wood.* In Saxon times a huge swathe of woodland stretched from Mundesley on the North Norfolk coast to Fersfield on the River Waveney.

Fig 5 View from St Mary's tower looking at the site of St Andrew's marked with a yellow cross, 2012.

If you climb the dusty spiral staircase of St Mary's tower (all 109 feet of it), you gain an amazing aerial view of Worstead, so good that the tower was used for Ordnance Survey mapping in 1882. The long narrow gardens of Honing Row beyond the Primitive Methodist Chapel (*4*) stretch from the street frontage to the back lane, which gives rear access and which once entered Church Plain through the entry beside St Andrew's Cottage (the room above the entry is a 1920s addition).

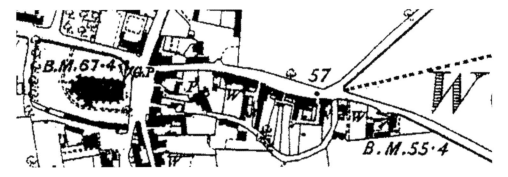

Fig 6 OS map 1886 Courtesy Norfolk Record Office

The gardens follow old boundary lines and at first sight their long narrow shape might suggest burgage plots. A burgage was a town 'borough' rental property, to use modern terms, owned by a king or lord. The property 'burgage tenement' usually, and distinctly, consisted of a house on a long and narrow plot of land with a narrow street frontage. Such burgage plots can often be discerned in the grain of the townscape of medieval boroughs. Burgage tenure did exist before the Norman Conquest, but burghers are absent from Worstead's *Domesday* entries. It is also emerging from archaeological studies in eastern England that the packing of dwellings so tightly along a street frontage was no earlier than the late eleventh century and that middle Saxon settlement was more dispersed, as are the hamlets of the parish of Worstead. The Worstead Enclosure Map of 1827 shows garden plots on much the same alignment, but wider than now, indicating subdivision after 1827. So it is unlikely that Honing Row was the first settlement in the parish, but the possibility that St Andrew's was the earlier of the two churches is mentioned in section 3 below.

Fig 7 Enclosure Map 1827 Courtesy Norfolk Record Office. Maps, C/Sca2/342

2. Worstead in the *Little Domesday Book*

At Christmas in 1085 King William the Conqueror (1066-87) and his Council decided to make a thorough survey of England to help them to meet the threat of invasion from William's rebellious son Duke Robert of Normandy and from King Cnut of Denmark. The survey was probably not intended to assess the country's wealth and make it available to the king in taxation, because how the *Domesday Book* is organised makes it a clumsy tool for collecting tax. More probably the royal intention was to assert political control over the king's tenants-in-chief and those who depended on them in the feudal system - that descending pyramid of land in return for service, military or agricultural. Commissioners went around each county asking questions about each landholding or manor in the time of King Edward the Confessor (1042-66) and in 1086, twenty years into William's reign. The answers collected from most counties were edited and written into the compilation known as the *Domesday Book*. The answers for the eastern counties were bound - unedited - into the *Little Domesday Book*.

Worstead has three entries under different spellings of its name: *Wredesteda*, *Vredesteda* and *Ordesteda*. These variations on the spelling of the name *Worstead* are three of twenty-five or more different medieval spellings. *Worstead Woven* (Ian Rendall 2000) explains the three variants as the attempts of educated scribes to make sense of the name Worstead as spoken by three different but illiterate people speaking in guttural Norfolk accents: the *W* in *Wrede* might be *UU* pronounced *OO*; the *V* in *Vrede* might be *U* pronounced as a long *U*; and the *Orde* might be *Orthe* if the *d* had a bar across its upright stem.

Wredesteda covers the lands owned by the Abbey of St Benet at Holme, founded in c.800 AD and refounded by King Cnut in 1019 or 1020. There is no mention of Worstead in Cnut's foundation charter, but by 1066 it and many other places in the Tunstead Hundred were in the hands of St Benet's. At that date St Benet's also owned *Ordesteda,* but by 1086 it had passed into the hands of Count Alan of Brittany. *Vredesteda* was a small estate held by Reynold, son of Ivo, in association with lands in Sloley and Scottow. The three entries below are translated from the Latin text of the *Little Domesday Book*. The translation appears in italics; suggested omissions appear thus *[there was]*; abbreviations are expanded thus *(in the time of King Edward)*; and explanations are given thus (a measure of land).

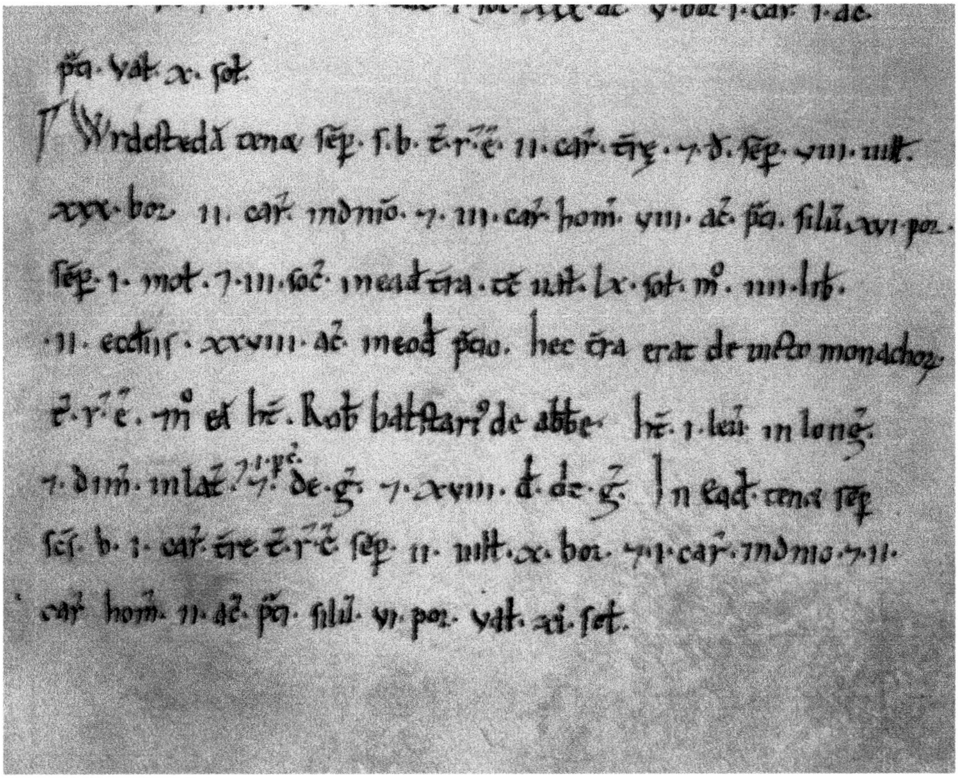

Fig 8 *Little Domesday entry for Wrdesteda transcribed below. Courtesy National Archives*

St B[enet] has always held Wredesteda TRE (in the time of King Edward); 2½ *carucates of land* (a measure of land in the counties of the former Danelaw, similar to a hide and likewise related to taxation, notionally 120 acres). *[There have] always [been] 8 villans* (*villans*, usually spelt *villeins,* were unfree peasants or serfs who usually held up to thirty acres each, but a survey of c.1270 suggests that more than twelve acres was rare in Worstead; so they were poorer than villeins in other areas where land was more plentiful)*, 30 bordars* (unfree peasants with less land, usually no more than five acres). *[There are] 2 ploughs* (plough teams of up to eight oxen and their plough) *in demesne* (the manorial lord's land farmed by unfree peasants in return for their holdings) *and 3 ploughs belonging to the men. [There are] 8 acres of meadow. [There is] woodland for 16 pigs. [There has] always [been] 1 mill. And [there are] 3 sokemen* (freemen obliged to attend the manorial court) *on the same land. Then* (before 1066) *it was worth 60s* (20 shillings made £1), *now £4. [The] two churches [have] 28 acres in the same value* (included in the preceding valuation?). *This land was for the* *sustenance of the monks TRE; now Robert the Crossbowman has it of the abbot. It is one league* (a variable measure, but more than a mile) *in length and half [a league] and one perch* (a variable measure, later standardised at 5.5 yards) *in breadth. And of the geld* (sic). *And [it renders] 18d* (pence: the silver penny, in Latin a *denarius*, was the only coin circulating in 1086) *of the geld* (land tax, assessed on the hide). *In the same [vill] St B[enet] has always held 1 carucate TRE. [There have] always [been] 2 villans, 10 bordars. And [there is] 1 plough in demesne and two ploughs belonging to the men. [There are] 2 acres of meadow. [There is] woodland for 6 pigs. It is worth 40s.*

St Benet held Ordesteda TRE; 2 carucates. [There have] always [been] 4 villans; [there were] 5 bordars, now [there are] 10. [There has] always [been] 1 plough in demesne and 1 plough belonging to the men. [There are] 2 acres of meadow. [There is] woodland for 6 pigs. It is worth 20s.

In Vredesteda [Reynold] also holds 3 acres.

3. The two Domesday churches

The *Domesday* entry for Worstead records two Saxon churches before 1066 and makes no difference between them. We know them as St Mary's and St Andrew's. Some fifteen Norfolk parishes have two churches in one *Domesday* entry, including Barton Turf, Hoveton and Wroxham. Were any as close as Worstead's two churches, separated by perhaps two hundred metres? The large size of the medieval parish of Worstead might suggest that it was the core of a larger *parochia* of a Saxon minster church, staffed by a team of priests. This is thought likely when eight or more smaller parishes share the boundary of a larger central parish (there are fifty-six such central parishes in Norfolk). Worstead has only six touching parishes: Dilham, Honing, North Walsham, Sloley, Tunstead and Westwick. The small parish of Tunstead has eleven conjoining parishes, and the much larger parish of North Walsham has fourteen. North Walsham has the remains of a Saxon flint church within St Nicholas' Church and is thus the more likely site of a minister. So one or both of Worstead's Saxon churches may have been a field church that broke away from its parent minster at an early date, perhaps helped by St Benet's Abbey which held lands in Worstead, North Walsham and other nearby parishes.

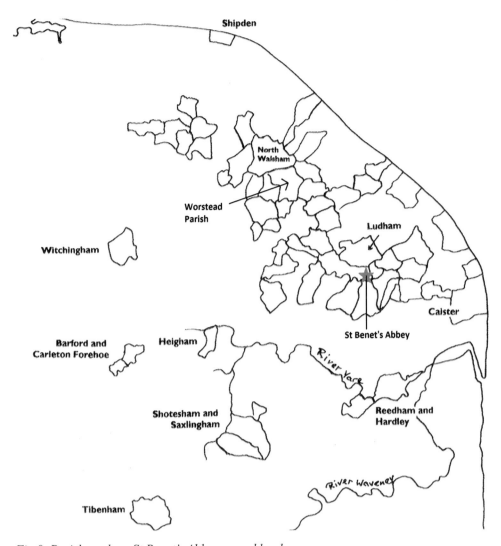

Fig 9 Parishes where St Benet's Abbey owned land.

St Andrew's (*11* - NHER 8208) may have been older than St Mary's, because a thirteenth century document names one of its holdings as the *Oldenkyrkewong* or the *Old Church's Field*. Both churches may have started as proprietary churches belonging to the lords of different manors. To be a thegn in late Saxon society - one who held land from a great lord or from the king - you needed five hides of land, a fortified house and a church. In 1954 human remains of possible late Saxon date (NHER 8184) were found to the south of St Andrew's. Local people also say that other skeletal material of unknown date was found and reburied as St Andrew's Close was built in the 1970s. If these remains came from its graveyard, St Andrew's may once have been independent of St Mary's, because parish churches like St Mary's did not usually delegate their burial rights to subordinate chapels. Whatever, St Mary's became a church with a parish and St Andrew's a chapel without a parish. A lack of records, especially before the Norman Conquest, hides what happened in Norfolk while parishes were gradually formed from late Saxon times to the late twelfth century. It may be that St Mary's gained its parish because it was the church of Worstead's most powerful manorial lord.

Fig 10 St Mary The Virgin Drawn by Mike McEwen © Worstead Parish Council.

St Andrew's was certainly called a chapel by the early years of Henry III's reign (1216-72). Before 1226 Sir Robert de Worstede granted the advowsons (the right to appoint the vicar), the rectorial tithes of St Mary's and St Andrew's and a lot of land to Norwich Cathedral Priory (see below, section 5). In 1226 Bishop Thomas Blundeville confirmed these gifts to the Priory, noting that they were to take effect after the deaths of John and Adam de Wurchestede. In his confirmation of 1256, presumably after the deaths of John and Adam, Bishop Walter Suffield made a clear distinction between the church (St Mary's) and the chapel (St Andrew's). According to Francis Blomefield (1805-10):

A manse or house was given to the vicar, with an acre of land, by the chapel of St Andrew, with all the altarage [burial and surplice fees] *of the church (except the tithes of the mills) and the rents of assize* [fixed rents] *belonging to the said chapel, and the oblations thereof; but if the oblations and profits of the said chapel exceeded five marks* [£3.6s.8d], *the remainder was to go to the prior and convent, and the vicar was to repair the said chapel, and to find all the ornaments, etc. The vicar was also to have the tithe of flax, hemp and other small tithes. It* [St Mary's] *was appropriated to the prior's table and to the cellarer of the said priory; but after this on the first day of April following* [1257?], *it was appropriated entirely to the prior's table* [its revenues were assigned to support the provisioning of the prior's table].

This arrangement was not unusual. The Priory was legally the rector of St Mary's, owned the right to collect tithes, and appointed a deputy, the vicar, to exercise the cure of souls on its behalf. As was normal, the Priory took the great tithes (usually a tenth of the grain crops), leaving the vicar with a house, the altarage and the small tithes. What kind of chapel was St Andrew's? Pilgrims may have journeyed through Worstead on their way to visit the Holy Rood of Bromholm Priory (a fragment of the 'true' cross), but there was no established pilgrim route through the parish that would have supported a pilgrim chapel. Nor was St Andrew's a chantry chapel, because the evidence of bequests to it is so limited. A parochial chapel was rarely so close to its parish church, but the best guess is that St Andrew's was just such a chapel, because it was put so firmly under the control of the vicar of St Mary's, and because those who left it money in the later Middle Ages were buried in St Mary's.

4. Deductions from Worstead's Domesday entries

The references to Worstead '*in the time of King Edward*' confirm the place-name evidence, indicating that there was a settled and organised society in the parish in the late Saxon period. That society seems to have varied little from that evident in 1086, even if some of its landholdings had changed. In 1086 there seem to have been three manors or landholdings in

11

Worstead: two in the first entry, one in the second; and perhaps a part of another in the third. We shall meet more manors below.

In 1086 St Benet's Abbey was still involved in the main manor or landholding of 2½ carucates in the *Wredesteda* entry, because Robert the Crossbowman then held it of the Abbey. Robert Ballistarius (Alblaster, Arblaster, or the Crossbowman) was probably a Norman who came over at the Conquest. It is likely that he held Worstead of the Abbey of St Benet at Holme for one knight's fee, though the knight's fee is not mentioned until the time of his son, Odo. The knight's fee meant that in time of war Robert was obliged to provide a mounted and fully-armed knight and his esquire for forty days, so that St Benet's Abbey could answer the king's summons to arms. Robert held other lands in Norfolk but Worstead was his main holding and his chief residence. His son Odo took the name 'de Worstede' which was variously spelt. The senior 'de Worstede' line died out in 1336, but the surname Alblaster was still in use in the early sixteenth century, not least on St Mary's rood screen and in the floor brasses of John and Agnes Alblaster. In 1066 St Benet's had held the advowsons (the right to appoint the priest) of the two churches noted in the *Wredesteda* entry, presumably the predecessors of the medieval St Mary's and St Andrew's, which shared twenty-eight acres of what medieval people called glebe land. This shows that both the churches were of Saxon origin, even if it is unclear in what century they were built. It is likely that Robert the Crossbowman held them in 1086, because the de Worstede family transferred the advowsons to the Norwich Cathedral Priory in the early thirteenth century.

In 1086 St Benet's still held the second and smaller *Wredesteda* manor or holding of 1 carucate, probably the Manor of Worstead St Andrew because the Abbey was paying its official there a shilling a week in 1272. However St Benet's had lost the *Ordesteda* manor of two carucates to Count Alan of Brittany, probably as a result of the Conqueror's displeasure at the strong support given to King Harold by Abbot Alfweald.

Is it possible to estimate Worstead's population in 1086? Alan Nash (*Southern History 10*, 1988) proposes these household sizes: six for priests, burgesses and villeins, four for bordars, and three for cottagers, freedmen and slaves. This suggests some 264 inhabitants, but the standard multiplier now used of 4.5 per man indicates just over 300. These totals may seem high until we realise that Norfolk was the most highly populated county in England in the late eleventh century.

Fig 11 Seed sowing from the Luttrell Psalter (Illustrated Lincolnshire 1320-1340) Courtesy British Library Board 2004

In 1086 Worstead's open fields must have covered at least 660 acres and probably more, depending on the size of the carucate or hide in north Norfolk; and there were ten acres of meadow. The 2,600 acres in the parish would have included the land kept in demesne by the lords of the manors to provide for the needs of their households. The open fields would have been divided into strips, let out to villeins and bordars in return for labour on the demesne. The villeins and bordars were unfree and bound to the land. Worstead's earliest map, the late eighteenth century copy of a map drawn in the late sixteenth century, suggests that late medieval Worstead was not a 'typical' three field village and probably never was: the map and some other sixteenth century references indicate nine open fields! This suggests that some hamlets in the parish had their own open fields. Open fields meant communal farming, using the ten ploughs drawn by teams of up to eight oxen each: heavy lands needed the full complement of oxen, but Worstead's lighter loams probably needed fewer. The crops probably included wheat, barley, rye, peas and vetch, but each open field would have lain fallow every now and again, in less fertile lands as often as one year in three. The corn would have been ground into flour at the mill mentioned in the Wredesteda entry. It was undoubtedly a watermill, for windmills were not introduced in England until the twelfth century and were not common until the thirteenth. Windmills were more powerful than watermills, but the wind had to blow! At least one of the mills mentioned in an ecclesiastical document of 1256 was wind-powered. The watermill was most probably at Briggate and powered by what is now the River Ant but which was then called the Smale:

the latter appears as an element in the place-name of the neighbouring village of Smallburgh.

Fig 12 Harvest from the Luttrell Psalter (Illustrated Lincolnshire 1320-1340)
Courtesy British Library Board 2004

Recorded livestock included up to eighty plough oxen and twenty-eight pigs. The pigs fed on beech mast and acorns in the woods. However, the meadow land, albeit only ten acres, indicates cows and maybe sheep. Geese and chickens were also probably kept. The meadows would be mown for hay before being turned over to livestock. The commons were an important resource for the owners of livestock. The late sixteenth century map, Faden's map of 1797, the Enclosure Map of 1827 and the Tithe Map of 1844 all suggest that there was much common land: a common heath in the north-west of the parish, merging into *Walsham Heath*; another common in the north (*Eastgate Common*) meeting with White Horse Common; common meadows in the north-east alongside the River Ant (*Limbo Marsh, Briggate Marsh* and perhaps stretching into *Horpeleye* (Orpley), where in c.1300 there was a turbary (the right to dig peat for fuel from common land) and in the south of the parish on either side of the tributary of the Ant (in the middle of Worstead Park as it is now); and other commons close to the southern boundary, verging on Sloley and Tunstead Commons. There were other small areas of common distributed across the parish. There would also have been some waste land.

This mixed farming was reasonably profitable: in 1086 the manors were valued at £4, £2 and £1 a year, not as much as the best manors, but by no means the worst. These values soon rose. Worstead's farmers were well placed to take advantage of an increase in the national population from some 2,000,000 in 1086 to between 4,750,000 and 6,000,000 in 1300. The increase led to a growth in trade and a rise in prices. There were markets for surplus production in Yarmouth and Norwich: both were accessible by water, certainly from Dilham and probably from Briggate; and there is evidence from Norwich Cathedral Priory that there was a considerable network of cartage between its manors and the Close. It seems there were few changes in farming technique. So for example illustrations in the *Luttrell Psalter* of the 1330s show that oxen were still used for ploughing; the seed was sown broadcast; and the crops were reaped with sickles.

5. Changes to the Domesday landholdings

The medieval landholdings in the parish - as in the Tunstead Hundred where Worstead lies and indeed across Norfolk - were so very complicated that they are hard to disentangle, but they have important consequences for Worstead's later history. Starting from the *Domesday* holdings we explore some of the changes that occurred up to the mid fourteenth century, taking much of the evidence from Martin & Setchell (2008).

The de Worstede family were generous in their giving to religious houses from their manor of *Wredesteda*. Odo and his son, another Robert, gave lands and a mill to St Benet's. Further down the family tree in the early to mid thirteenth century, Sir Robert (the third Robert), transferred the advowsons of St Mary's and of St Andrew's to the Norwich Cathedral Priory: an 'extent' (a valuation survey) of about 1270 recorded that with St Mary's went the rectory manor of twenty-eight acres of land with a further 114 acres, three messuages (dwellings) and six cottages held by its tenants; and with St Andrew's went thirty acres of land and one acre of meadow and a further two acres and three cottages held by tenants. Sir Robert and his successors also gave lands to the Priories of Pentney (Augustinian), Hempton (Augustinian) and Bromholm (Cluniac), and to the Carbrooke Preceptory of the Knights Hospitaller of St John. The grant by John de Worstede to Pentney Priory (probably in 1256) was substantial: a carucate of land, a messuage, a mill, rents worth 50s, ten acres of wood with the whole pond of Worstead and Crowbeck, and the whole alder carr (marsh). Although the manor, valued at £8.10s.4d in 1328, was regranted by the Prior to John for life, it was still in Pentney's possession at the dissolution of the Priory in 1537. Hempton's manor in Worstead was valued at £4.8s.11d, but at what date is unclear. Bromholm's manor in Worstead was valued at 104s.2d again at an uncertain date but perhaps in 1428.

*Fig 13 The Miller from the Luttrell Psalter (Illustrated Lincolnshire 1320-1340)
Courtesy British Library Board 2004*

The survey of c.1270 shows that Philip de Worstede kept only twelve acres in demesne and let out the rest of his fifteen hundred acres to twenty free tenants, hereafter primary tenants: thirteen were laymen and seven were religious foundations. The twenty primary free tenants had their own villeins and secondary free tenants. Of the 1,377.65 acres, the villeins had 438.5 acres and 103 secondary free tenants had 939.15 acres. Of the 103 secondary free tenants, twelve occupied half the land and the rest had holdings with a mean size of 4.8 acres, well below the level needed for subsistence - a point to which we shall return in Section 5 below. Many of the twenty primary free tenants were probably soon seen as lords of separate manors, because the *Nomina Villarum* (the *Names of the Manors*) survey of 1316 lists eighteen lords in Worstead and Westwick, while *Kelly's Directory* of 1902 notes twenty manors in the parish of Worstead alone. In the early fourteenth century, Nicholas, son of Philip de Worstede, gave what remained of his lands and rights to St Benet's Abbey. They passed to the bishop of Norwich in 1536.

The history of the landholdings in Count Alan's manor of *Ordesteda* is even more complex and are here simplified. In 1273 Oliver de Ingham held a knight's fee in Ingham and Worstead of Robert de Tateshall. By the mid fourteenth century the Stapleton family had acquired this holding through marriage and in 1378-9 and again in 1392-3 they gave land in Worstead to the Trinitarian Priory of Ingham, which they had founded in 1355-65. Part of the Ingham holding was sub-let to the le Gros family, for in 1344 Oliver le Gros held half a knight's fee of Oliver de Ingham in Worstead and Westwick, in addition to another half fee held of the Barony of Rye in Sloley. By 1336 the senior line of the de Worstede family had died out and the le Gros family (probably originally from Normandy but first recorded in England during Stephen's reign, 1135-54) were the major landowners in Worstead.

The survey shows how complex landholdings might be. Six of the twenty primary free tenants also had holdings as secondary or tertiary tenants: for example, Reginald le Gros (father of Oliver - see above) was a free tenant with 124 acres but also a subtenant of William de Mauteby for fifty acres and of William de Stalham for ten acres. Some of the subtenants had quite a number of holdings: for example Henry de Brokele had eight in seventeen acres; Eustace de Worstede had six in seventy-two; and Ralph le Spencer had five in nearly twelve. In all there were 155 holdings: 12% of them contained 60% of the land in holdings of 20 to 90 acres; 7% of the holdings contained 11 to 20 acres, and 17% 6 to 10 acres. So only 36% of the holdings were of six acres and above, leaving 64% of the holdings containing five acres or less, and 43% one acre or less. Why was this so? Because north-east Norfolk was the most densely populated part of England, there was a huge demand for land that could not be met. Partible inheritance may have contributed to the emergence of such small holdings: instead of a holding passing to the eldest heir, it was divided between all the heirs, creating holdings that were well below the ten acres needed to provide for a household's needs. If households needed to find other sources of income and if worsted weaving provided one, this might explain why the cloth industry developed in Worstead and in the towns and villages north of Norwich. In the longer term, the small size of most medieval holdings had a knock-on effect: if the cloth industry were to decline without another source of income being found, former weavers would have to become landless labourers and work for the minority who held large holdings. These possibilities will be further explored below.

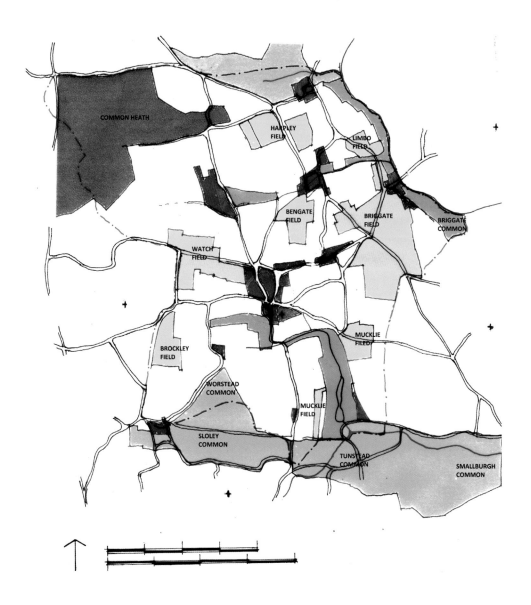

Fig 14 Land Use within the parish during the Middle Ages

Dark Blue	=	*Tenements*
Light Blue	=	*Riverside Common*
Green	=	*Common Woodland*
Brown	=	*Common Heath*
Yellow	=	*Common Fields*

2. WORSTEAD IN THE LATER MIDDLE AGES

1. The naming of worsted after Worstead

Worsted cloth takes its name from Worstead. It is first called the *cloth of Worstead* in the City Chamberlain's accounts of 1301 when some of it was presented to the Assize Judges in Norwich. The rolls of the Norwich Cathedral Priory record that in 1309 its Chamberlain bought 381.5 ells of the *cloth of Worstead* for the monks' summer habits (an ell was 45 inches). Such purchases may have begun as early as 1297 and they continued after 1309, for example 218 ells in 1318 and 300 ells in 1331. These City and Priory records suggest that worsted cloth was already identified with Worstead. So the parish was certainly weaving the cloth commercially in the thirteenth century and quite possibly in the twelfth. Also the earliest act in the House of Lords' Record Office (*The Taking of Apprentices for Worsteads in the County of Norfolk* of 1497) uses the present spelling of the village. To name a cloth after its place of manufacture was common. North Walsham cloth was said to be of a finer texture than that of Worstead. Walsham and Worstead cloths were both sold at St Ives Fair in the mid fourteenth century. The cloth of Aylsham, also presented to the Assize Judges in 1301, may have been a linen known as *Aylsham web*, but later on Aylsham cloth combined linen and worsted. *Dilhamsay* was another variety of worsted from a neighbouring village.

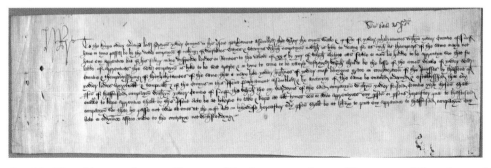

Fig 15 The oldest act kept at Houses of Parliament archives, Westminster 'The taking of apprentices for making worsted (woollen yarn) in Norfolk'. 1497. © Parliamentary Archives, London; .HL/PO/PU/1/1497/12H7n1

The cloth to which Worstead gave its English name originated long before the parish appeared on the map of Norfolk. People first began to herd wild sheep in about 9000 BC in the Fertile Crescent, formed by the rivers Tigris and Euphrates in modern Syria and Iraq. The oldest surviving cloth, a piece of linen excavated at Catalhoyuk in Turkish Anatolia, dates from c.6200 BC. The earliest commercial weaving of wool was probably part of a growing specialisation of craft skills in the cities of the Fertile Crescent soon after 4300 BC. Cloth of the type we call worsted was first woven in Babylon and Egypt soon after 2000 BC. The Romans learned to weave it from the Egyptians and called it *trita*, meaning *smooth* or even *threadbare*. The Romans probably brought it to England after 43 AD. By then Britons were already weaving cloth: eighty-nine weaving combs of 150-60 BC were excavated in the Iron Age lake village of Glastonbury; and weaving combs of similar date have been found in East Anglia. Roman Britain made and exported fine woollens, woven from the short staple wool of Soay sheep, then the predominant breed. To produce long staple wool, wool with long fibres suitable for making *trita*, Soay sheep were crossed with a Roman long-wool breed. Finds of spindle whorls, wool combs and loom weights testify that the people of Saxon and Danish Norfolk also wove cloth, seemingly both woollens and worsteds.

Fig 16 Spinning Thread and Weaving, from a rare record of frescoes from Thebes, recorded 1819-1822 on his second visit to Egypt by Frederic Cailliaud (1787-1869) The Stapleton Collection

English wool had a good reputation in medieval Europe, especially in Flanders, but raw wool was a less profitable export than finished cloth. So from time to time kings banned the export of raw wool to encourage cloth production. Even so, some 10,000,000 fleeces a year were exported around 1300 and raw wool still accounted for 74% of customs revenue in 1421. However, by 1100 London and then Huntingdon, Lincoln, Oxford and Winchester had enough commercial weavers to require regulation by local craft guilds. What of Norwich or even Worstead?

It has been claimed that Flemish weavers introduced the cloth they called *ostade* to Worstead. Blomefield's *History of Norfolk* (1805-10) says that Flemish weavers came to Norfolk soon after 1100 and that '*some settled at Worstead*' and '*introduced the art of stuff-weaving there.*' This claim has been repeated many times, but Blomefield offers no evidence. *Stuffs* were the superior worsted fabrics, created in the sixteenth century and also called the *new draperies*: they were not the simpler worsteds made in Worstead. Then in 1271 King Henry III invited foreign weavers to England, exempting them from all taxes and duties for five years. Again no evidence shows that any came to Norfolk, let alone Worstead. The *cloth of Worstead* was an established brand by 1301 and it probably took a century or more to attain that status. Before then we have no proof that any of the weavers in the parish were Flemings. So worsted weaving in twelfth and thirteenth century Worstead was probably a skill handed down from the Romans, Saxons or Danes. The place-name Worstead is an early usage, suggesting that the cloth was named after the parish, not that *worsted* was a Norfolk rendering of the Flemish *ostade.*

Did Flemish weavers contribute to worsted manufacture in Norwich or in Worstead after 1301? King Edward III (1327-77) married the Flemish Philippa of Hainault and invited Flemish weavers '*to exercise their mysteries in the kingdom.*' A law of 1337 promised that '*all cloth-workers of strange lands, of whatsoever country they be, ... shall come safely and surely, and shall be in the King's protection and safe-conduct, to dwell where they will.*' Soon Flemings settled in Abingdon, Bristol, London, Winchester and York. Did some come to Norwich? One John Kempe had already come to England to teach weaving in 1331: was he the John Kempe de Gaunt (Ghent) who settled in the parish of St Peter Mancroft in Norwich in 1333? Quite possibly. Records in 1375 and 1391 show aliens living in the Norwich parishes of St Giles and St Andrew, the traditional cloth-making area. Assaults on

Dutchmen (that is, foreigners) occurred at much the same time in Norwich, and Flemings were murdered in King's Lynn and in Great Yarmouth in 1381. Were these aliens unpopular because they were immigrants or because they wove worsteds, when fourteenth century Norwich mostly wove woollens from the short staple wool of the local sheep? Their numbers were small, because the subsidy rolls (records of parliamentary taxation) rarely list more than a dozen foreign families in fifteenth and early sixteenth century Norwich.

The crafts and industries of Norwich were regulated by guilds, which protected customers against defective wares, punished poor workmanship, defended producers from the competition of untrained labour, and often set prices and wages. The guilds oversaw the masters who owned their tools and machines, bought their materials and sold the products of their work-shops; the journeymen who were skilled craftsmen employed by masters for a daily wage; and the apprentices who were bound by indenture to masters while they learned the mysteries of their craft. Did some Flemish weavers then try to evade regulation by the city's gilds by moving out of Norwich, even to Worstead? It is possible, but no evidence places any of them in the parish. Some suggest that we should look for Flemish, Dutch and Walloon surnames, such as Goost, Kemp, Kempster, Kypp, Kypper, Rump and Skypper, but we know few Worstead names until the parish registers begin in 1558. The Strangers, who arrived after 1565, dwarfed the numbers of all previous immigrants (see Chapter 3).

2. Farming and famine before the Black Death

Worstead's soil is good, mostly well-drained silty loam (roughly 40% sand, 40% silt and 20% clay), but with a more sandy loam on the plateau in the north-west corner and a more peaty loam in the valleys of the River Ant and its tributary streams, where the water table is high. This fertile soil had the potential to bring prosperity to medieval farmers.

In the thirteenth century some 70% of a peasant's diet - largely bread, pottage and ale - came from crops grown locally, often on his strips in the open fields, for which he paid by performing a variety of tasks for the lord of the manor. In the early thirteenth century many demesnes (lands kept for his own use by the lord of the manor) had been leased out. However from the mid century most were taken back into direct management by the lord, because the potential for profit increased as prices rose and wages fell or remained static. By 1300 most manorial lords, ecclesiastical and lay, managed their demesne lands themselves. So for example from the 1250s Norwich Cathedral Priory derived up to 80% of its grain requirements from its manors, and made up the shortfall by buying from corn-mongers. They in turn purchased grain directly from lay demesnes, or - especially during years of shortage - by resorting to local markets despite their higher prices. In 1300 Norfolk probably had England's most productive and progressive farming economy. It specialised in growing barley, producing high quality malt: barley tolerated drought better than other grains in this driest of English counties. So 70-80% of the arable land in the demesne of the Worstead manor of St Benet at Holme was sown with spring barley. Oddly the Worstead manor of Norwich Cathedral Priory (Amners St Andrew) did not directly supply the monks. Its main crop was winter wheat, but legumes (peas, beans, clover, etc.) were also grown to fertilise the soil for the wheat crop and provide forage for livestock and pottage for the peasants. The Priory's manor was run by six or seven servants: a reeve, two or three ploughmen, a carter, a cowherd and a dairymaid.

Fig 17 Medieval harrow team, Luttrell Psalter (Illustrated Lincolnshire 1320-1340) Courtesy British Library Board 2004

However a mini ice age struck England soon after 1300 and lasted until the late seventeenth century. It caused what has been called the Agrarian Crisis of the early fourteenth century. Dreadful weather in 1314-16 and in 1321 led to harvest failures and famines in 1315-17 and 1322-23. These famines may have reduced Norfolk's population by 10-15%, though it then resumed its rise up to 1349. In 1319-20 the Great Cattle Pestilence also killed some 62% of English cattle. Farmers began to replace oxen with horses, because they were up to 50% more efficient as draught animals, a process already started in Norfolk once an effective horse collar was invented in the thirteenth century. Inevitably prices rose and trade in farm produce was also hampered by a coinage which carried far too much clipped and counterfeit money. Those on fixed wages suffered severely. Thefts of grain doubled. Hungry people sought other sources of income, furthering the growth of worsted weaving.

3. The Black Death of 1349

Fig 18 Victims of the Black Death from the Toggenburgh Bible 1411
Courtesy Wikimedia Commons.

Recent scientific analysis of skeletons from plague cemeteries across Europe shows that the Great Plague (known as the Black Death since the nineteenth century) was bubonic plague, caused by the bacterium *Yersinia pestis*. The plague swept across Norfolk in the spring and summer of 1349. People were terrified because there was no cure. Some fled, but others turned to the church and its sacraments, hoping to appease the God who, most believed, had sent the plague to punish sin. England's population, some 4,750,000 to 6,000,000 by 1300, fell to below 3,000,000 by 1377. Mortality rates varied, but the more dense the population the higher was the death rate. Norwich, which may have had 25,000 citizens by 1349, was probably reduced to about 8,000. Many of Norfolk's rural parishes lost 30-40% of their people, but nearby Coltishall 55%. Worstead would have fared well if it lost only a third of its parishioners. Priests were especially vulnerable. More than 800 priests in the Norwich diocese died in 1349-50: the institution of William de Atterton as Rector of Westwick on 20 May 1349 was quickly followed by that of Richard de Tutterbury on 4 July. The plague returned, if less severely, in 1361-2, 1369, 1374-5, and then roughly every twenty years until 1665. Some of these outbreaks seriously depleted the population, by 10-15% in 1471 and up to 20% in 1479-80. Plague was not the only killer, only the most serious. That the plague inspired real fear over a long period is revealed by a description of the burial of Edmond Themylthorpe who '*dyed 12th March 1653 of the Plague in the evening and was buried the next morning, with only two men carrying him.*' After the plague Norwich recovered quite well, though its population only reached some 11,000 by 1500. Did the decision to rebuild St Mary's only thirty years later in 1379 mean that Worstead was doing well? Or were its parishioners trying to placate an angry God?

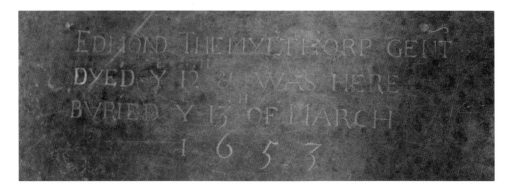

Fig 19 Edmond Themylthorpe's tomb in St Mary's chancel

Traditional open field farming was badly disrupted by the Black Death because experienced leaders and workers died. Many tenants, free and unfree, who owed their lord rent or labour services were no more, and crops and animals were left unattended. So there were poor harvests in 1349-51. Thereafter landowners saw their profits decline, as prices fell for lack of buyers and wages rose for lack of labourers. The average wage of a carter before 1349 was 1¾ d. a day but 2¾ d. after 1349, but rates varied widely: in Worstead two extra carters were each paid 6¾ d per day for four days' work in 1357, while the four regular carters were paid 4d per day each for the thirty days of the harvest. The four no doubt felt aggrieved! The fall in grain and livestock prices was not immediate but became pronounced and long-lasting from the mid 1370s, helped by high yields in 1376-99. Thereafter prices tended to fluctuate. Falling prices combined with rising money wages made the direct cultivation of the demesne less profitable. So between 1380 and 1420 many lords returned to the policy of leasing out their demesne. In an age of shortages, price fluctuations and lack of coin, most rents were fixed in grain (most often in malted barley, which was 25% lighter but 15% more valuable than the raw grain). At the same time a dependence on the market in grain became more pronounced, with many large-scale buyers choosing to purchase grain direct from the demesne or farm rather than in public markets. Other manorial lords turned to sheep, at least temporarily, because sheep provided wool, milk, meat and manure, lived on poorer land than cattle, and needed less labour. So the high point of England's trade in raw wool was the fifteenth century, but by then Worstead had been turning wool into worsted cloth for at least two centuries, adding considerable value to the raw wool.

Many landlords tried to re-establish the relationship with their peasants as it had 'always' been, using the courts - at least initially - to enforce the obligations of serfdom and the pre-plague wage levels established by the Ordinance of Labourers of 1349 and the Statute of Labourers of 1351. Peasants thought that the Statue was unfair, because the royal justices appointed to enforce the statute were invariably landowners themselves, were entitled to keep a sixth of the fines they imposed, and sometimes paid their own workers more than the legal wages, while punishing others who did so. Half the cases brought before the Norfolk justices in 1575-79 were for breaches of the Statute. However, despite the law, campaigns of passive resistance and the flight of villeins from their manors caused the money wages of peasants and of craftsmen to rise by about thirty per cent in 1350-80. Real wages of peasants also began to rise from 1376 and they could afford to eat more meat and more wheat bread and less of the inferior barley or rye bread. In reality the peasants knew that they now held more bargaining power than ever before and their increasing confidence may have emboldened them to take part in the Great Revolt which spread across much of southern and eastern England in 1381.

4. The Great Revolt of 1381

Most historians, including most recently Juliet Barker (2014), now speak of the Great Revolt or the English Rising of 1381, not of the Peasants' Revolt. This is because a good half of the rebels were not peasants, but craftsmen (particularly weavers and other cloth workers in Worstead), tradesmen, minor clerics, officials and even a few gentry.

Fig 20 Extract from John Speed's Map 1611 Courtesy Cambridge University Library

Many of these were townspeople, who were as resentful as the peasant rank and file of excessive market tolls and of restrictions on their freedom to buy and sell, especially when the whole economic life of a town was subject to the exploitation of overmighty monastic houses, as it was in Bury St Edmunds and in St Albans. Some contrasted such great wealth and power in the Church to the simple life of Christ and objected to the holding of the chief offices of state by senior clergy: the Chancellor was Archbishop Simon Sudbury of Canterbury (born c.1316), and the Treasurer was Sir Robert Hales (born in c.1325), Grand Prior of the Order of the Knights of St

John in England (both were killed during the Revolt). Some of the lesser clergy, who as stipendiary priests and chantry chaplains held no benefice, were found among the leaders of the Revolt. John Wrawe, who led the rebels in north Suffolk and influenced events in Norfolk, was one, as was the itinerant John Ball or Balle, a radical preacher widely regarded as heretical by church authorities. His part in the Revolt is uncertain but the monastic chronicler Thomas Walsingham of St Albans put words into his mouth that have resonated down the ages:

When Adam delved and Eve span
Who was then a gentleman?

There is little evidence that the 'commons' - as the rebels called themselves - aimed to overthrow the social order: they sought to end the vested interests and corrupt practices that they saw in the conduct of government, the administration of justice and the assessment of taxation. The Hundred Year's War with France, renewed in 1369, was going badly and the Good Parliament of 1376 blamed the king's ministers for poor leadership and the mis-spending of taxes. As a result the unpopular John of Gaunt (1340-99), Duke of Lancaster and the rich and powerful uncle of King Richard II, was excluded from the Government. Even so, more taxation was needed and Parliament's solution was the poll tax in 1377, 1379 and 1380. The four pence a head levied in 1377 was a penny less than the daily wage of a skilled worker and a penny more than that of a labourer. In 1379 a graduated poll tax was levied. In theory it was fairer but most people found themselves paying more than in 1377: a salaried chaplain who paid four pence in 1377 now paid two shillings. Despite further military failures Parliament granted a third poll tax in 1380 that required twelve pence (one shilling) at head. This demand came after a bad harvest and during a very harsh winter. Returns to the Exchequer showed that the number of eligible tax-payers in Norfolk had fallen from 88,797 to 58,714 (other counties recorded similar falls). The government assumed that there had been widespread tax-evasion and appointed commissions in many counties to reassess the poll tax and enforce payment. The Norfolk commissioners made another 8005 people pay the tax. Naturally the Sheriff, Justices of the Peace, other local officials, lawyers and gentry who profited from their membership of the commission became hated figures who were often targeted by the rebels. The reassessment was the final straw that led to the Revolt of June 1381.

Fig 21 & 22 Two of the crosses commemorating the 1381 battle site
Drawn by Mike McEwen, © Worstead Parish Council

The peasants, the other half of the rebels, also objected to the poll tax but had other grievances. They sought freedom from the bondage of serfdom. A serf was tied to the land and could not leave it for more than for a day without his lord's permission. He had to pay rent and also work on the lord's demesne for one to three days a week. He also had to pay when for example he inherited his father's holding; when his son or daughter married; when he registered the sale, exchange or lease of a piece of land; when he infringed the 'custom of the manor' as he farmed his strips in the open fields; or failed to use the lord's mill to grind his grain. Such fines and fees were enforced, often arbitrarily, by the manorial court, from which serfs, unlike freemen, had no appeal. Most unfree peasants were not opposed to the king's law but objected to private jurisdictions like the manor court. They also wanted freedom to agree their wages by negotiation and to pay no more than four pence per acre in rent. So the peasants aimed to seize and destroy manorial records from gentry houses and monasteries to deprive the courts of the evidence they needed to enforce serfdom and limit wages under the Statute of Labourers. Records were burned at fifty-six Norfolk places and incidents were recorded at ninety-five. Many manors of the unpopular John of Gaunt were attacked, and records were also destroyed at manors belonging to St Benet's Abbey. A minor incident occurred at Worstead: was it perhaps the gathering of some supporters of Geoffrey Litester?

Geoffrey Litester or Lister led the rebels in north-east Norfolk. His surname, variously spelt, indicates that he was a dyer. He was called *Galfridus Lestere* in the poll tax return of 1379, when he paid six pence, and his goods, confiscated after the Revolt, were assessed at 33s.9d. His dyeing business was in Felmingham, but was described as '*of Worstead.*' Did he live in or own the dwelling now named Geoffrey the Dyer House (*3* - NHER 17024) or - more likely - its fourteenth century predecessor? His leadership group included two other Worstead men: Thomas Skeet and William Kybyte (or Cubitt). Skeet, not a wealthy man, paid four pence in the 1379 poll tax. Kybyte, described as a clerk in minor orders, had goods in Worstead worth sixty shillings and paid 2s.6d poll tax for his wife and himself: if he were a stipendiary priest he would have paid 3s.4d. and should have been unmarried. These two were joined by John of Trunch and Sir Roger Bacon of Baconsthorpe, the only one of the Norfolk gentry to admit joining the rebels voluntarily, who had just returned from war in Brittany with four men at arms and five archers.

The 'commons' in north Norfolk were gathering as the Revolt in the south-east was collapsing after the killing of Wat Tyler at the second meeting of the king with the rebels at Smithfield on 15 June. Crucially the 'commons' believed that they were not rebels but loyal subjects and had royal approval to act against traitors and corrupt officials. King Richard II, though only fourteen, had met the rebels at Mile End on 14 June and granted almost all of their demands: the right to seize all traitors; the abolition of personal and tenurial villeinage and of serfdom; a rent of four pence per acre; employment by free contract; and the liberty to buy and sell as they chose without paying tolls. Richard promised that letters enshrining this agreement would be drawn up and sealed with the Great Seal; that each county represented should have a banner of the royal arms; and that all would be pardoned if they followed their banners back home. It looked as if the rebels had won, though the Statute of Labourers was not repealed nor was the poll tax revoked. However his councillors persuaded the king to retract his concessions on 2 July, but Richard had granted them in good faith, for in November 1381 he asked Parliament to root out the causes of the Revolt and offered to abolish villeinage. The royal letters and banners convinced many in the counties, including some officials and some gentry, to join the effort to end corruption in the conduct of local administration.

Fig 23 Geoffrey the Dyer House Drawn by Mike McEwen, © Worstead Parish Council

On 17 June Litester mustered his forces on Mousehold Heath, where Sir Robert de Salle was killed, perhaps as a negotiator for the city but more probably as a fugitive. After entering Norwich the rebels had the discipline not to loot and burn the city, but they began to administer justice as they saw it. Reginald de Eccles, an over-keen Justice of the Peace, was captured and executed. The houses of four prominent citizens were looted and their records burned: Archdeacon William de Swyneflete deputised for the bishop in his absence, while Henry Lomynour JP, Walter Bixton and John Fychet had been involved in collecting the poll tax. Four knights were made to serve Geoffrey Litester as he held court in the Castle. Two may have been the Sire de Scales and Sir Thomas de Morlee, but the other two were Sir

John de Brewes, a former Sheriff, and Sir Stephen de Hales, MP for Norfolk in 1377 and 1380, Sheriff in 1378-79, and a JP from 1380. Both had sat on the poll tax reassessment commission. On 18 June Litester, Bacon, Skeet, Kybyte and Trunch led a large group from Norwich to meet Suffolk rebels at Beccles, entered Great Yarmouth and destroyed a hated charter giving the burgesses rights over the trading of fish within a wide area of the coast. On 19 June the rebels looted the properties in Yarmouth and Caister of Hugh Fastolf and William Elys, both impeached for corruption in the Good Parliament of 1376 and involved the collection and reassessment of the poll tax. The rebels also organised the destruction of manorial records at Carrow Abbey, West Dereham Abbey, St Benet at Holme Abbey, and Binham and Bromholm Priories and at many individual manors held by these monastic houses, Bury St Edmunds Abbey and Norwich Cathedral Priory, and by Bishop Henry Despenser, John of Gaunt, John de Brewes, and other lords.

Bishop Henry Despenser of Norwich is sometimes described as the Fighting Bishop because he had fought abroad before he became a bishop and later fought in a crusade. Absent from Norfolk when the revolt broke out, he soon returned with - says Walsingham - eight 'lances' and a few archers to stiffen the landowners' resolve (a 'lance' often meant an armoured knight and his esquire). News of his approach may have caused the rebels to send delegates to win royal approval for their actions and a pardon to plead against Bishop Despenser. Thomas Skeet, William Kybyte, and John Trunch took with them John de Brewes and Thomas de Morlee who were expected to negotiate an audience with the king. At Icklingham the party met Bishop Despenser, who executed Skeet, Kybyte and Trunch at Wymondham. On 23 June the rebels mistakenly thought Despenser had reached St Benet's Abbey and tried to storm it, but were repulsed. In fact Despenser arrived in Norwich on 24 June and he caught Litester and his dwindling group on 26 June on the heath where the boundaries of Worstead, Westwick and North Walsham meet. Litester's men had no weaponry that could resist the attack of even a small number of mounted and armoured knights. Thomas Walsingham modelled his story of a pitched battle on an account of Boudicca's defeat in 61 AD, itself written far away from the event by the Roman historian Tacitus. John Capgrave (1393-1464), the Augustinian Prior of Lynn, wrote later, but probably more reliably, that the rebels soon surrendered when Despenser promised them safe conduct home. Did the bishop intend to punish the leaders, not the led? Some rebels were killed, maybe including Litester, though one report said he was found hiding in a cornfield and executed. We know of some 1200 named rebels in Norfolk and Speed's Map of 1611 says - improbably - that Litester '...*led fiftye thousand Souldiers into the field...*' However it seems that only thirty-four were killed in the skirmish or executed after it, while sixty-one were pardoned. An inquest held at Worstead by John Rede or Reed in January 1382 found that William Kybyte and Thomas Skeet, Richard Hobbeson and Geoffrey Coleman of North Walsham, Thomas Radbote of Sco Ruston and Robert Smyth of Ridlington had indeed been killed in June 1381. Of these Kybyte and Skeet had, as we know, been executed earlier at Wymondham. So folk memories of many dead are exaggerated, but Bishop Despenser marked his victory by erecting four memorial crosses at each corner of the battlefield. One stands on Worstead's north-western boundary and another fragment is nearby (*40*). The Bishop may have commissioned the fine altarpiece or retable of the 1380s that graces St Luke's Chapel in Norwich Cathedral, though the heraldry round its border suggests that it may have been a thanksgiving gift from Norfolk gentry to the Bishop for his leadership during the Revolt.

Fig 24 'Henry le Despenser' by Amitchell125 at English Wikipedia - Own work. Licensed under Public Domain via Wikimedia Commons

On 23 June commissioners were appointed to suppress the uprising in Norfolk and Suffolk. They included some who had suffered at the hands of the rebels, notably the Sire de Scales, John Brewes and Stephen de Hales, who were scarcely impartial and made some arbitrary judgements. There was little resistance left by the time they began work, though there was an unsuccessful plot in September 1382 to seize Bishop Despenser and other magnates and to occupy St Benet's Abbey perhaps as a base for a further uprising. After the withdrawal of the concessions granted by the king at Mile End, the 'commons' were liable to prosecution for rebellion but in November 1381 pardons were granted - at a price - to many rebels, though 287 named individuals were excluded. Pardons were also extended to those who had acted arbitrarily in suppressing disorder. Quite a number of those whose property had been stolen or destroyed sued for damages, but no new private prosecutions were allowed after July 1383.

Bishop Despenser's victory did not solve the problems faced by landlords after the Black Death. Serfdom was not abolished by law as the rebels had asked. Very few lords freed their serfs, like William Septvans of Kent did in his will of 1407, and the demand of Kett's Rebellion in 1549 that the Duke of Norfolk should free his villeins proves that serfdom lasted in some measure into the sixteenth century. However outright refusals to perform labour services or passive resistance that undermined their value meant that serfdom gradually withered away. This process was accelerated by the fall in grain prices which caused many landowners to lease out their demesnes, though they found that many tenants shunned lands to which labour services were attached. As labour services came to be replaced by rents, the traditional, communal farming of the open fields became less attractive, and subsistence farming was slowly replaced by production for a developing market in towns.

5. The town of Worstead

In the twelfth and thirteenth centuries England became increasingly urbanised: in 1300 some 15% of England's population lived in towns. By then Norwich had some 15,000 people, but other Norfolk towns probably had fewer than a thousand. The survey of c.1270 (Chapter 1) indicates that Worstead was indeed a town. Most medieval landholdings in the parish were below the ten acres needed to feed a family, so that many families needed a livelihood to replace or at least supplement what they could grow on their few acres. So the spinning and weaving that had once provided for household needs probably became a cottage industry that offered worsted cloth to a wider market. What they earned from making cloth could then be spent buying food and other necessities at the local market.

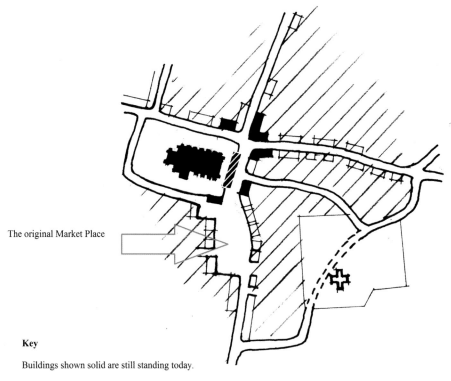

The original Market Place

Key

Buildings shown solid are still standing today.

White hatching shoes the range of a Tudor building, drawn by John Starling c1840 (demolished 1842)

Buildings in outline only are taken from plots as shown on the first map of Worstead by Robert Wymer a 1781 copy of a late 16th century original by Edmund Thurston of Norwich.

Fig 25 Suggested plan of the late medieval Town Centre c 1500.

Further evidence for Worstead's urban status comes from its tax records. As early as 991 AD Worstead was assessed at 18d. for the Danegeld - the same as North Walsham. In 1334 its tax assessment of £14.10s.1¾ d was the nineteenth largest in Norfolk, behind North Walsham's assessment of £15. To put that figure in perspective, Norwich was assessed at £97 at a time when its population was climbing towards the 25,000 that it may have attained just before the Black Death in 1349. Worstead lost taxpayers in the plague, so that its assessment in 1449 was lower at £12.10.11¼ d. Even so, it ranked fifteenth in Norfolk's assessment, ahead of North Walsham's assessment of £11. Then Worstead's poll tax return in 1379 indicates that worsted weaving was its main industry. The return identifies forty-five *websteres* (a *webster* was a worsted weaver) among the 282 taxpayers in the parish. This compares well with the forty-six weavers in North Walsham's poll-tax return of 1380-81. In both places the weavers relied on other textile workers, woolcombers, spinners, dyers and the like: many of Worstead's 282 taxpayers were probably involved in cloth making. Nearby villages had fewer weavers: Witton had seven, Ridlington six, Smallburgh and Crostwight three each. There were numbers of other craftsmen and tradesmen among Worstead's taxpayers in 1379, including three *taillours*. If Worstead was typical of East Anglia, about four-fifths of those who paid the poll tax were wage-earners who did not earn their living from farming.

The poll tax was paid by people over sixteen in 1379 and it is estimated that some 40% of the population was under sixteen. So Worstead's 282 adult taxpayers should have been 60% of the town's population, giving a total of 470 inhabitants of all ages. However some of the adults would have been poor enough to count as beggars, who were exempt, and there were doubtless some tax-evaders. So the figure of 470 inhabitants can be regarded as a minimum. This suggests in 1379 that Worstead was still a town of reasonable standing, despite losing a significant proportion of its people in the Black Death. It is likely that at least 670 people lived in the parish the early 1340s.

6. Worstead's market

Worstead's medieval economy depended on farming and on the making of worsted cloth, but the buying and selling of food, goods and services extended more widely. As befits a town, Worstead had its own market (*10* - NHER 41157, 40820, 40937). It was one of 283 in Norfolk on the eve of the Black Death in 1349, evidence of a rise in commerce and trade based on money transactions and on credit. Oliver le Gros, the lord of manors in Worstead and Sloley, obtained a royal charter for the market in 1336. The market day was then Tuesday, but as it was '*to the hurt*' of Sutton market owned by Earl William de Clynton of Huntingdon, it was changed to Friday in 1339. A second market day on Saturday was added in 1340, but it was forbidden in 1358 because it was detrimental to Aylsham Market, owned by Queen Isabel. Earl William and Queen Isabel evidently had the ear of the king! Evidence from the time of the Great Revolt suggests that buyers and sellers at the market would have resented the tolls charged by Oliver le Gros.

HOUSE DRAWN BY JOHN STARLING

Fig 26 The building that once stood on the corner of Church Plain and Westwick Road.

Church Plain was once narrower than it is now, because a fine house stood on the west side of Church Plain near the corner of Westwick Road, with an inn and brewery on the same side to the south. The house, drawn by John Starling, dated from the sixteenth century or very possibly earlier, judging by the large size and off-centre position of its chimney. It had an eighteenth century facade with Flemish crow-stepped gables and was demolished in 1842. So the actual market place was between Front and Back Streets, although the commercial centre must also have extended to the probable shop in the undercroft below St Andrew's Cottage (see section 8 below). In 2005 an archaeological dig across the island between the streets (NHER 41157) found no evidence of buildings between the late Iron Age and the late seventeenth century, nothing between an Iron Age ditch and eighteenth century post holes. Worstead was settled before 1066 and we might expect to find late Saxon and early medieval buildings in its centre between the two churches. So did a customary market already exist in what became the medieval market place? A royal charter was sometimes granted for a pre-existing customary market. The idea is intriguing, and the fact that all the surrounding markets except Sutton were in existence by 1275 adds weight to it.

Fig 27 The original market was held on the island on which the Old Post Office now stands. A row of buildings stood where the cars are parked in the right foreground.

In our mind's eye we need to remove the present day Old Post Office, Clemsea House and Jasmine House. Imagine the empty space filled with market stalls, some of which may have become wooden or even brick built sheds before the market came to an end when an outbreak of the plague led to its removal to North Walsham in 1666. Laburnum Cottage in Back Street probably began as a single storey cottage in the seventeenth century and gained an upper storey in the late eighteenth, but its front rests on a medieval wall which may have bounded the market. The last house in Back Street sits on what appears to be a continuation of that boundary wall. Both the Old Post Office and Clemsea House seem to belong to the late seventeenth and the eighteenth century. How and when did they evolve from the wooden stalls and sheds of the market? Their architectural history is worthy of further exploration: the rear wall of Clemsea House suggests that it includes elements of three former properties.

7. The manufacture of worsted cloth

Worsteds are made from long staple wool (wool with long fibres), unlike woollens which are made from short staple wool (wool with short fibres). Traders called wool-broggers brought the long staple wool by packhorse from west Norfolk, from Lincolnshire and Leicestershire, and by the eighteenth century from as far afield as Westmorland and Ireland. The jingling of harness bells would have been a familiar sound as the packhorses entered Worstead. In later times the wool came already combed and spun, but this brief account of worsted manufacture starts from the newly-sheared fleece.

The preparation of the wool involved *sorting* the long from the short staple wool; *willeying* or beating with rods, often of willow, to remove dust and disentangle the locks; *picking* to remove any foreign bodies left; *scouring*, often in a fulling mill, to remove grease, and/or *washing*.

Fig 28 Worsted wool comb. Courtesy www.waysofthewhorl.wordpress.com

The long staple wool was then *combed* (short staple wool for woollens was *carded*). Two combs were used: each had about thirty long tapering teeth (by the eighteenth century the best were of tempered steel) set at right angles to the handle. One comb was fixed to a post and the wool was hung on it; the other was used to pull through the wool to lay each hair parallel and to separate the long wool from the short (the *noils*). The *sliver* containing the long fibres was wound into a ball called the *top*, ready for drawing and spinning. A comb pot or small charcoal stove was used to heat the comb to make it run through the fibres more easily. It was hard work and the comb pot gave off noxious fumes.

Combed wool was then *spun* into yarn. Early spinners used a *distaff* and a *spindle*. The spinner drew a lock of wool from the combed *top*, attached it to the *distaff* and twisted it with the help of a pendant or *drop spindle*, which had a *whorl* fixed to its lower end to act as a flywheel. The *spinning wheel*, introduced into England in the thirteenth century and improved with a foot pedal in the mid eighteenth, was used for woollen yarn, but not for worsted for several centuries. Even the most skilled worker could not spin worsted yarn of even quality, and spinning was slower than weaving, so that looms might be idle for lack of wool, especially in the summer when the women and children who did the spinning worked in the fields.

Scouring might again be used to remove the combing oil from the yarn. *Dyeing* preceded weaving if the yarn was to be *dyed in the wool*, as was the case for patterned worsted stuffs. If the cloth was to be *dyed in the piece*, as was the norm with plain worsteds, then *dyeing* followed weaving. Until the nineteenth century vegetable dyes were used: *oak bark* (brown), *madder* (red and orange), *saffron* (yellow and orange) or *woad* (blue).

Fig 29 Spinning and carding yarn, from the Luttrell Psalter (Illustrated Lincolnshire 1320-1340) Courtesy British Library Board 2004

Yarn that was to be used as the *warp* (the lengthways thread) was *twistered* (given an extra twist) on a *twistering mill*, often in the weaver's workshop: this gave it added strength. *Weaving* began with the thread (the *weft*) wound on a spindle. The longitudinal *warp* threads were fixed to the loom. The spindle was thrown through the *shed* created as alternate *warp* threads were raised and lowered. The weaver then used *slay* or batten to push each thread up of *weft* up against the weaving already on the loom. A narrow loom could be operated by one weaver but a broadloom needed two to propel the *shuttle* from side to side. Even the best weavers found it hard to achieve a uniform texture. The tall warp-weighted vertical loom was gradually replaced by the more costly treadle, horizontal or shaft loom , which was used for longer, wider and patterned pieces.

Finishing involved mending any defects; *dyeing* if the yarn had not been *dyed in the wool*; and *calendering* or pressing with a variety of irons and rollers depending on the finish required. Worsteds did not require fulling as woollens did.

8. Weaving and the cloth trade in medieval Worstead

We have some evidence of medieval weavers, spinners and dyers in the parish. The earliest named were Edmund the Quilterer and Bartholomew the Teynturer: the French *teinturier* means dyer. Together they assaulted the Worstead bailiff in 1299, resenting his insistence that as villeins they must work on their lord's demesne. In 1329 a commission investigated the protests of weavers against the appointment of an alnager or inspector of worsted cloth: it tried the cases of seven worsted weavers from Worstead and ten more from six neighbouring parishes: were Worstead's weavers either more militant or more numerous than elsewhere? Probably the latter. The commission's conclusions are unknown, but King Edward III revoked the alnager's licence - a victory for protest. We have also learned above that there were forty-five *websteres* in 1379 and that Geoffrey the Dyer was the leader of the Great Rising in north Norfolk in 1381.

Worstead specialised in plain worsteds, in black monks' or canons' cloth and in furnishing cloths such as *say* or *serge*. John Paston I (1444-1503) provided testimony to the quality of worsted cloth, though his often-quoted praise applies more widely to Norfolk. On 20 September 1465 he wrote from prison in London to his wife Margaret:

Fig 30 Older vertical looms were still clearly in use in the 16th century. Image Courtesy Worstead Woven © Worstead Parish Council

I pray you ye will send me hither two eln [ells] *of Worsted for doublets, to hap me* [wrap me up warm] *this cold winter, and that ye enquire where William Paston* (probably his uncle) *bought his tippet* [cape] *of fine worsted, which is almost like silk, and if that be much finer than ye should buy me, after seven or eight shillings, then buy me a quarter* (of a yard = nine inches) *and a nail* (2.25 inches) *thereof for collars, though it be dearer than the tother, for I would make my doublet all Worsted, for worship* [for the glory] *of Norfolk.*

Less often quoted is her reply a week later:

I have do spoke for your worsted, but ye may not have it till Hallowmas (All Saints' Day on 1 November)*, and then I am promised ye shall have as fine as may be made. Richard Calle* (the Pastons' steward) *shall bring it up with him.*

We have little evidence of the premises in which worsted was woven in the Middle Ages. No medieval weaver's cottage survives in Worstead, because most cottages were poorly built of timber, wattle and daub, or clay lump, and were roofed in thatch. Their sites now lie under more modern buildings or under the fields on either side of Vicarage Lane as far as the lane running between the Old Vicarage and the School. The low sun reveals humps and bumps that suggest buildings in the meadows west of Vicarage Lane; and in the hot, dry summer of 1976 the crop marks of buildings and roadways became visible in the fields north of Westwick Road and Honing Row.

Fig 31 Brass of Thome Whatt

Probate records indicate only a dozen weavers in Worstead between 1370 and 1857, but few other than master weavers left enough property to require a will. Master weavers were first evident in the fifteenth century. They often owned the looms, supplied the materials, paid the weavers for their skill and labour by the piece, and sold the finished cloth. The present Manor House (*2 - NHER 17023*) began as a fourteenth century hall and added a weaving loft in the fifteenth century, sadly converted to bedrooms in the twentieth. The loft was probably the workshop of a master weaver and had space for a dozen looms and a cubicle for the supervisor. Other master weavers leased looms to weavers who worked at home, supplying the materials and paying for the woven cloth by the piece. Master weavers became people of independence and substance, but they did not achieve the wealth of the merchant-clothiers, who supplied the long staple wool and sold the cloth for a good profit. One Thome Whatt (Thomas Watt?), weaver, died on 16 August 1506 and was interred beneath a brass in front of the rood screen in St Mary's. He was however no journeyman weaver: only a master-weaver could have afforded such a prominent tomb.

One of Worstead's worsted merchants was identified in the 1480s by Edmund Paston II, who urged William Paston III, then barely 21, to consider as a potential wife...

a widow of Worstead, who was wife to one Bolt, a worsted merchant worth a thousand pounds [who] gave his wife a hundred marks in money, household stuff, and plate to the value of 100 marks, and £10 a year in land. She is called a fair gentlewoman. I will for your sake see her. She is full sister, by both father and mother, to Harry Inglose. I propose to speak with him, to get his good will. This gentlewoman is about thirty years, and has but two children; she was his wife but five years.

Mr Bolt left a capital of more than £1000, roughly equivalent to £500,000 today, when most waged labourers took home £2 to £4 a year!

Fig 32 The undercroft of St Andrew's Cottage

Around 1400 another merchant built the fine brick-vaulted and groined undercroft (*7* - NHER 19461, listed II*) that lies beneath the seventeenth/eighteenth century St Andrew's Cottage. The elaborate style of the undercroft looks more ecclesiastical than secular, but we can discount any connection with St Mary's or St Andrew's. It has often been said that it was used to store wool in the cool, but its street frontage and the fine workmanship of its vault (chamfered brick rendered in lime plaster and then lime-washed) suggest that its owner intended it to be seen. So it was probably a shop, perhaps displaying the goods of a worsted merchant. The undercroft now has two bays and measures 7.5 x 2.9 metres, but it appears to have been extended to the rear, perhaps to create a second access: the roof behind the last arch slopes upward and the rear wall is not original. The north wall has a now-blocked access from the original house above. The ground level outside has risen considerably since 1400. So there would have been fewer steps down to the undercroft than now, it would have seemed much less of a cellar, and the doorway would have let more light into a very white interior. It may not be as grand as the undercroft of Robert Toppes' Dragon Hall in Norwich, but it still indicates real wealth in medieval Worstead.

At least one of the many fourteenth century London mercers who came from Norfolk was a Worstead man: mercers dealt in luxury cloths, often foreign, but also those woven in north-east Norfolk. Somewhat later in 1471 John Paston II refers to '*a worsted man of Norfolk, that sold worsted in Winchester.*' Yet most of Worstead's cloth would have been sold in Norwich. The city became a staple town for trade in wool and cloth under Edward III (1337-77) and by the mid fifteenth century it produced more worsted than woollen cloth. In 1388 the Norwich authorities established the *worstedseld* (north of Market Place and opposite the Guildhall's main entrance) to check all worsted cloth and seal it before it could be sold only by enfranchised citizens. The *worstedseld* did not last beyond 1414 but the city kept control of the worsted trade, although the guilds regulated the individual crafts. Norfolk's worsted production was disrupted by the Black Death (1349-51), by the Great Revolt (1381), by the Hundred Years' War (1337-1453) and by the Wars of the Roses (1455-87). However worsted merchants redirected their exports away from war-torn France to the Hanseatic League in North Germany and the Baltic, and to the Low Countries, using the ports round Norfolk's long coastline. By 1515-20 there was a sixfold increase in trade, but by then most of cloth went by the wagon-load to London, where many Norfolk cloth seals have been found.

9. The creation of St Mary's Church

The St Mary's (*1* - NHER 8209) that we now see began life in the early fourteenth century, but it was extensively remodelled between 1379 and 1512. It has been described as one of East Anglia's great wool churches, but it is not as grand as Long Melford or Lavenham. Yet its Perpendicular exterior is in Norfolk's top ten and in 1955 it was given a grade I listing as a building of exceptional architectural and historical interest. It is part of the great rebuilding which saw perhaps two thirds of England's churches rebuilt or substantially altered in the English (as opposed to the Norman or French) Perpendicular style of the late fourteenth to the early sixteenth century.

Fig 33 St Mary the Virgin, from the south east. Worstead 2012

Our understanding of St Mary's architectural history is by no means complete. We know nothing of the St Mary's that existed for some time before 1066 and for two or three centuries afterwards. Was a Saxon timber church later replaced by a Norman flint and limestone church, because the use of limestone in Norfolk generally postdates the Norman Conquest? However some things are clear from the interior of the church. The nave arcades with their octagonal pillars and hollow-chamfered arches date from the early fourteenth century. The original fourteenth century roofline of the nave and the door that gave access to the roof's rafters are visible on the wall above the high tower arch: the nave had grand proportions even then. However the exterior is more informative.

Fig 34 St Mary's interior looking at the base of the tower.

The tower - 109 feet high - was in place when the nave was built. So it belongs to the fourteenth century but was embellished in the fifteenth. Its square windows replaced earlier windows and those in the north and south faces have tracery in the form of a rose with five petals, probably the Virgin Mary's 'rose without a thorn.' The rose also appears on the de Worstede coat of arms: which came first, the dedication to St Mary or the family's coat of arms? The two flushwork friezes in the base of the tower and the unusual blank flushwork arcading above are typical of the fifteenth and early sixteenth century. Flushwork is an ornamental exterior surface in which knapped flints are combined with shaped freestone to create a variety of patterns: Stephen Hart (2000) likens it to inlaying in cabinet-making. The flints were knapped into squares, rectangles, rounds and leaf shapes. Although the church's construction layers have been lost thanks to modern efforts to combat the damp, occasional finds of struck flakes show that knapping took place on site: flushwork was costly because it was labour intensive. St Mary's also has a good deal of flushwork on the aisles, but some flints are now missing, especially on the north side of the church. They are found every so often when earth is disturbed nearby, sometimes with the medieval lime mortar still attached.

Fig 35 Typical flushwork along the external plinth.

The aisles extend beyond the nave into the chapels of Our Lady and of John the Baptist, which partly embrace the chancel. The aisle windows are Perpendicular, with alternating styles of tracery. North of the chancel is the two-storey vestry: in about 1450 Isabel Borough left property in North Walsham to finance its construction. The clerestory with ten Perpendicular windows on each side was raised in the late fifteenth century, for William

Cosby left 6s.8d in 1480 for '*the new roof.*' Two flying buttresses were added on each side to support the clerestory and absorb the sideways thrust of the new single hammer-beam and arch-braced roof.

Fig 36 The hammer beam roof and clerestory windows of the late 15th century

The two-storey south porch was probably built in the later fourteenth century, but elaborated in the fifteenth. The parapet above the external arch has a chequer-board frieze in flint flushwork. Above the archway are three niches for images. The present image of the Virgin Mary is Victorian. In the Middle Ages church dedications to Mary quite often linked her with two other saints. Which two saints flanked Mary's medieval image? They may have been St John the Baptist and St Thomas of Canterbury, to whom the side chapels were first dedicated. Inside the porch the vault has a central boss showing the coronation of the Virgin (the Virgin kneels between the Father and Son). It is surrounded by bosses of the four Evangelists. The stone benches remind us that medieval marriages took place at the church door, before the couple entered the church for the nuptial mass: Chaucer writes '*husbands at the church door had she* [the Wife of Bath] *five.*' The stair to the porch's upper chamber is in the angle between the south wall of the nave and the west wall of the porch, and is accessed by a door inside the church. Was the chamber used to store documents and records; was it the vicar's study and library; or was it a schoolroom for a few pupils taught by a chantry priest, who was also paid to offer masses for the souls of the departed? Perhaps all three. The porch was restored as a memorial to King Edward VII who died in 1910.

When John Kynneburle was Worstead's vicar *'the chancel of this church was new built.'* This rebuilding began in 1379, only thirty years after the Black Death. Whether it was motivated by the need to appease God or to glorify him, the reconstruction over the next century and half was not needed to accommodate rising numbers. It absorbed resources that farm labourers and worsted weavers could ill-afford and that the wealthy might have devoted to the relief of poverty and suffering, as some Protestants did after the Reformation. We need all our imagination to enter into the mind-set that gave us St Mary's. The rebuilding of 1379-99 cost £24.4s.4d. As the legal rector the Cathedral Priory contributed thirteen oak trees from Plumstead Wood and more timber from St Leonard's Wood.

Fig 37 The interior viewed from the ringing chamber

In the 1480s the chancel was severely damaged by fire. The Priory was involved once more, making another gift of oaks in 1485, as recorded in the Cellarer's rolls. For his work on the 'new' chancel master mason John Antell, who had worked on King's College Chapel in Cambridge in 1459, was paid 74s.9½d in 1484-5. Carpenter Andrew Couper was paid 61s.10½d. for making the new roof in 1485-6. Other payments were made for glazing three chancel windows in 1487-8. Beside the priest's door in the chancel's southern wall are the weathered remains of two sundials. One may have charted the time by the sun's summer position, and the other by its winter position. These scratch or mass dials gave the approximate time for mass. Often a line was scored more deeply to give the usual time but sometimes a ring of holes allowed a peg to denote a variable time. St Mary's did not gain a clock until 1768.

An inn was reputedly built for the masons who were then working on St Mary's in the late fifteenth century. An inn and a brewery were included in the buildings that straddled the present churchyard wall on the west side of Church Plain: the sunken path that once ran between the church and the buildings is still visible in the churchyard, running north from the Heritage Map. This inn may be the one known by the early nineteenth century as the Sign of the Lemon, because its name is old: *Lemon* tried to make sense of *leman*, when this medieval word for sweetheart was no longer in use.

Fig 38 The path between the church and the 'Sign of the Lemon'

Not only was the Cathedral Priory involved in the rebuilding of St Mary's but three men with variations on the surname de Worstede were monks at the Priory. John de Worstede became the Priory's Communar in 1323-30 and in 1338-9, and had much to do with the rebuilding of the cloisters. William Worstede was the Prior in 1427-36: he was a frequent attender at Bishop Alnwick's trials of Lollards in 1428-31, and was active in the Benedictine Chapter in the Province of Canterbury, serving as one of its four delegates to the Council of Basel in 1435. Robert Worstead was less distinguished: at a visitation of 1514 he was accused of begetting a child on a girl from the city! Also a Reginald de Worstede was instituted as Vicar of Coddenham in Suffolk on 28 July 1349 during the Black Death.

10. The medieval interior of St Mary's

The rood screen and the other screens of St Mary's are its crowning glory, but their story belongs to Chapter 3, because they replaced earlier medieval screens in the early Tudor period. There are two mysteries associated with these earlier screens. In the 1950s the northern chapel housed two loose panels which depicted St Peter's with his keys and possibly St Matthew with a *tau* (or T-shaped) cross, sometimes described as St Anthony's cross. Did they come from a screen that enclosed the choir on either side of the chancel, for some fixtures for such a screen survives on the northern arch? And where are they now? And a piece of wood was once inserted into the wall below the west window of the north aisle. It was inscribed: '*Pray for the sowles of Jonh-s Mack and Isabel hys wyfe the whech have [borne] thee cost of thys werk.*' The work is purported to be one of the chancel screens, perhaps the precursor of the Alblaster screen.

There is much evidence that enables us to imagine St Mary's in its medieval splendour. The church would have been full of colour. In the sunlight the small Victorian blue and red panes in the clear glass of the windows now cast a fraction of the rich glow that was once emitted by the medieval stained glass. We do not know what stories were portrayed in the glass to a mostly illiterate congregation, but they were extended onto the walls. There were wall-paintings of St George and the dragon and of St Michael and the devil; and perhaps one of St Christopher bearing the Christ Child on the north wall opposite the south door. A doom painting on the chancel arch would have warned unrepentant sinners of eternal, fiery punishment after death. Little paint now remains. There are fragments of a painted pattern on the southern pier of the chancel arch and on the easternmost arch of the nave's southern arcade. Roundels painted on either side of the sanctuary may be consecration crosses, and another roundel containing a 'T' in the northern chapel may signify its former dedication to St Thomas of Canterbury. That dedication became impolitic in Henry VIII's reign and his image is the one most damaged on the northern parclose screen. So the Chapel of St John the Baptist, formerly in the south, may then have moved to the north, and the southern chapel became the Lady Chapel. Sir Robert Camounde, priest, willed that '*his goods be sold and all the said* [south] *chapel be paved with marbyll stone up to the grave of John Ovy*' and Walter and Isabel Borough gave a pew for the same chapel. In his will of 1493 John Sparhawk asked to be buried before '*hey altar newe made*' on the north side of the church: if he meant the altar in the northern chapel, the move may have taken place earlier than Henry VIII's reign.

Fig 39 Small fragments of original decoration remain.

Images of the saints were placed near the altars of medieval churches, often to the north. In the northern chapel the plinths on which they stood remain north and south of the altar. Plinths for images in many windows of the north and south aisles were probably associated with nave altars: there were at least nine altars provided by guilds or chantries. Two of the guilds were dedicated to Our Lady and to St Thomas, for Agnes Watts who died in

1529 was a benefactor to them. Another guild was dedicated to St John the Baptist. Candles would have been kept burning before the images.

Fig 40 Font and its cover counterbalance - inset top left

The octagonal font of the fifteenth century stands on three raised steps before the western screen. In 1461 William Eche left 15s. for its cover, which was practically rebuilt in 1954: its pinnacle alone retains the original gilding. As the cover is raised, a counterbalancing angel - sadly now wingless - descends from the roof above. The broken font bowl that sits outside the south door is not the remains of a previous font: a letter from George Smith, published in *The Woven* (No. 12, August 2013), shows that it once belonged to St Bartholomew's Church in Sloley.

There are other small reminders of medieval devotion. Two holy water stoups survive, one beside the door into the north aisle, the other beside the priest's door into the chancel. In the south aisle there was a banner-stave locker, now filled in: processions played a large part in medieval ritual. The wooden roofs have some magnificent bosses, even if they are now missing most of their medieval colour. Many are clearly Christian, others perhaps more pagan, including several Green Men. The term 'Green Man' was coined in 1939 for the representation of a man's face wreathed in foliage or with foliage emerging from his mouth. Green Men originated in pre-Christian mythology, but became common in churches from the eleventh century, though the earliest so far found - in a church near Poitiers in France - dates from the late fourth or early fifth century. Medieval people may have seen Green Men as symbols of Easter or of eternal life, but they remain mysterious, like the many grotesques that appear in churches, such as the gargoyles on St Mary's tower. A Green Man, visible in a roof boss at the west end of the north aisle, is unique among St Mary's carvings in being rough or unfinished, and yet it is full of cheeky character. It became the logo of Worstead's Heritage Trails in 2012. The roof bosses would benefit from further recording and explanation.

Fig 41-44 Some of St Mary's green men, two of which still retain some original colour

Memorial brasses remind us of the importance that medieval people put on praying and saying masses for the souls of the departed, so that they might be released from the pains of purgatory and ascend into heaven. In the chancel is the figured brass of John Yop, Rector of Booton, who died in 1399, left money to repair the church and asked for burial outside the priest's door into the chancel. Another figured brass in the chancel is that of Sir Robert Camounde, priest, who died in 1482 ('Sir' was the courtesy title used for a non-graduate priest). Also in the chancel are the inscription brasses of Xtopher (Christopher) Rant and Joanne his wife (1428) and of Johannis Spicer (1450). The brasses before the rood screen include those of John and Agnes Alblaster; Thome Whatt (Thomas Watt?), weaver, who died on 16 August 1506; '*Johannis Carman, 26 July, Anno dom 1518*' with his merchant's mark below; and '*Johis Gladenet, Isabelle his wife, died 21 Dec AD 1507.*'

Fig 45 Johannis Carman's brass with his merchant's mark

Near the south door is the brass of '*Rog[er] Blome*' which was originally sited near the chancel door: he left £10 for the '*new bell*' in 1493. Brasses once existed of Isabel, wife of Walter Borough; Jeffrey Dey and Oliver Wythe in the southern chapel; and Thomas Wilkins, Alderman of Norwich and Sheriff in 1486, in the south aisle. Over twenty indents remain of brasses removed in the sixteenth or seventeenth century. Two show an outline of a chalice and wafer, signifying a priest. Another shows a heart and three scrolls indicating that the person died elsewhere and his or her heart was sent home in a lead casket for burial beneath the slab. The two stone covers from chest tombs, now at the west end of either aisle, have uncertain dates and have been moved from their original locations. A fragment of a helmeted effigy (NHER 58019) lies outside the church in the angle of the porch's west wall and the south aisle's wall. Made from costly Purbeck limestone, first used in churches in the thirteenth century, its smooth surface suggests it may originally have been polished. It is likely that it was part of a tomb slab sited in the church. So of whom was it the effigy? Who ordered its removal from the church? When was it moved? The story continues into the twenty-first century in Chapter 8.

Fig 46 The helmeted effigy (NHER 58019)

To imagine the medieval interior of St Mary's we must add the colour mentioned above, spread either by the sunlight or the candles glinting on the images of the saints. Then we must remove the pews, for there only a few benches and most people stand. The straw or rushes on the earth floor rustle as people move about. The damp, the burning wax and tallow, and the incense scent the air. Mass is celebrated in Latin, which most do not understand, by one from the incomplete list of St Mary's medieval vicars:

Warin de Testorton (1256)
John (1299)
Edward Johnes (1304)
Peter de Reynham
William de Aldeby (1346)
Oliver de Wytton (1353)
Roger de Felthorp (1355)
John de Kynneburle (1365)
Edmund Martin (1386)

The priest is dressed in rich vestments and uses liturgical vessels of high quality (see Chapter 3). Everyone kneels as the priest raises the paten and chalice above his head at the elevation, the most sacred point of the service. The mass holds sacred power, because it is believed that by a miracle the bread and wine become (in substance but not in form) the body and blood of Christ. However, the people do not take communion: they do that once a year at Easter, after serious preparation in Lent that includes confessing to a priest and performing a penance.

11. Church Cottage and the graveyard of St Mary's

Did Church Cottage (*16* - NHER 47652) ever have any connection with the church, apart from its name and position? Was it perhaps the 'church house' - a medieval version of the nineteenth century church hall? From the south and east its much altered structure seems to belong to the early eighteenth century, but the brick and flint section of the north wall is medieval. The retaining wall by the cottage shows that the churchyard has risen by more than a metre since the Middle Ages; but then Church Plain was lower by at least a metre than it is today, so that the rise may have been more than two metres. As many as 20,000 bodies may have been interred in the churchyard before its closure in 1918

Fig 47 Church Cottage. Note ground level of churchyard is above sill height.

3. TUDOR AND STUART WORSTEAD

1. St Mary's in its pre-Reformation glory

Fig 48 Chancel Rood Screen

Traditional parish religion was at its most elaborate in the half century between Henry Tudor's victory at Bosworth in 1485 and Henry VIII's Reformation that began in 1533. Some of St Mary's early Tudor splendour, survives in its screens. The hard-to-read Latin inscription on the rood screen of 1512 lacks its first words, but they are easily supplied. A literal translation reads: *[John Albaster] and [Agnes] his wife caused this screen to be built, on behalf of whose souls may God be propitiated, amen. This work was made and finished in the fifteen hundred and twelfth year of our Lord, to whom be glory, praise, honour and hymns. Amen.* John Alblaster probably derived his name from *arblaster* or crossbowman and he was descended from Robert the Crossbowman who held the main manor of Worstead from the abbot of St Benet at Holme in 1086. John may have made money from worsted, because he left a loom to one John Dykins. He also gave £1 to help a kinsman of Mr Berde, the parish priest of Worstead, through university. When John died in

1520, he bequeathed £7 to the fabric of St Mary's (to be paid in yearly instalments of £1) and a stipend of £6 a year for five years to '*an honest priest*' who '*should sing and pray for my soul and all my friends' souls.*' His tiny memorial brass, in front of the screen, has a conventional representation, not a portrait. His wife Agnes died in 1524. She left bequests to charity, including 12d. and other goods to '*the blind woman, Mother Kove.*' Agnes' brass has an inscription but no image.

The rood screen lacks its loft, rood beam and rood (the figure of Christ on the cross flanked by the Virgin Mary and St John), though Starling's manuscript of 1838 reports: '*A truly magnificent carved and gilded rood beam that stood about five feet above the great screen was removed at the time of the restoration in 1809.*' The ledges that supported it are visible on either side of the chancel arch. Twelve of the rood screen's sixteen pictures, six either side of the rood doorway, are among the finest in East Anglia: they were little damaged in the sixteenth or seventeenth century. The twelve central images depict the disciples, each displaying his symbol. From north to south they are

St James the Less with his fuller's club
St Philip with his basket of loaves
St Simon with his fish (Simon was the brother of Jesus and although not
    strictly an apostle he often replaces Judas Iscariot on rood screens)
St Jude with his boat
St Matthias (?) with his purse
St John with his chalice from which a dragon emerges
St Andrew with his saltire cross and book
St Peter with his key and book
St James the Great as a pilgrim with his gown, staff and scallop shell
St Thomas with his book and lance
St Bartholomew with his flaying knife and book
St Barnabas with a rather strange background of roses (he was wrongly
    labelled as St Jerome in the nineteenth century).

Fig 49 Central 12 saints: north to the left.

The two outermost pictures on the north side of the rood screen are not medieval. A note appears in Starling's manuscript: '*The two figures ... on the panels had been defaced... I then painted with my own hand the Saviour and St Paul to complete the series. What figures had been there I cannot tell; what I supplied is by conjecture. W.T.S.*' The initials were those of William Tylney Spurdens, Master of the Paston School (1807-25) and Curate of Worstead (1837-40).

Fig 50 North pair

Fig 51 South pair

Did he also paint the two outermost figures on the south side? If so, he probably repainted what was already there, because the two rather crude images depict medieval saints who were improbable choices in the nineteenth century. Both owe more to legend than history. St William of Norwich (portrayed with a crown of thorns, three nails and a knife in his chest) was a twelve year old boy found murdered in Thorpe Wood on 23 March 1144. Thomas of Monmouth, who arrived at Norwich Cathedral Priory a year or two later, heard the rumours surrounding the death, and wrote *The Life and Passion of St William.* He cast the Jews as the villains of the piece, alleging - without evidence - that they murdered William in a ritual that parodied Christ's crucifixion. This anti-Semitic fiction, called the 'blood libel,' was not known in England before this date. William is rarely depicted on screens, only here and at Litcham, Loddon and Eye. And why in 1512, when the Jews had been banned from England since 1290 (they were not readmitted until 1655); and when William's shrine in Norwich Cathedral was attracting relatively few pilgrims? The second image is St Wilgefortis who appears bearded, crowned, and tied to a cross. Legend has it that she was a Portuguese princess who dedicated her virginity to God and who rejected her pagan parents' choice of husband, the King of Sicily, by praying for and growing a beard. Naturally her suitor rejected her and so her father crucified her! Her cult probably originated in fourteenth century Flanders, and may have been brought to Worstead by Flemish weavers. In England Wilgefortis was called St Uncumber, because, it was said, she would 'uncumber' unhappy wives of tiresome husbands, if they offered a peck of oats and lit a candle for a year and a day before her image. The Worstead statue, which probably stood by one of the nave altars, and another from Boxford in Suffolk were destroyed in Edward VI's reign, but one survives in Henry VII's Chapel in Westminster Abbey.

Fig 52 North parclose screen   *Fig 53 South parclose screen*

On either side of chancel arch are the parclose screens for the northern chapel of St John the Baptist and the southern Lady Chapel. The paintings probably date from the fourteenth century and are of good quality, if in need of some conservation. The northern screen depicts St Lawrence with his gridiron; St Thomas of Canterbury, vested as an archbishop; St Bartholomew with his flaying knife; and St Philip with his basket of loaves. The southern screen features St Peter with his keys; St Paul with his sword; St John the Baptist with his lamb; and St Stephen vested as a deacon with a book. Close examination suggests that they were two halves of one screen cut to fit their present positions. The point at which the rood stair emerges from its late fourteenth century turret in the north wall is too low for the screen in its undivided state. So it is unlikely to have been the precursor of the Alblaster screen. Was it then transferred from St Andrew's in the mid sixteenth century? It seems likely (see section 3 below).

Fig 54 The Tower screen

The western screen set in the high tower arch virtually reproduces the parclose screens. Its inscription reads: '*This werke was made in ye yer of God MCCCCCI* [1501] *at ye proper cost of ye catell of ye cherche of Worstead callyd ye bachellers' lyte* [light] *ye God preserve with all the benefactors of ye same now and ever, Amen. Then wer husbonds* [wardens] *Chrystofyer Rant and Jefrey Dey.*' It was not unusual for the bachelors or maidens of a parish to support a light (a candle kept burning before an image in the church), nor for them to do so from the proceeds of *catell* or cattle, for medieval parishes might keep cattle or sheep as a way of raising money. The screen's images were repainted in 1831 (see Chapter 4).

2. Changes to St Mary's during the Reformation

Henry VIII's break with Rome made the Church *in* England into the Church *of* England with the king as its Supreme Head, changed the succession to the throne and ushered in an age of rapid religious change. Evangelical Protestants, called Puritans from Elizabeth I's accession to the restoration of Charles II, wanted to purge churches of all anti-Christian 'popery' - the Pope, priests, monks and nuns, the mass, the cult of the saints, purgatory and intercessions for the dead, and more. They were hampered by the fact that Henry VIII rather liked the mass, but he did bring the English clergy to heel, dissolve the monasteries, reduce the cult of the saints, and authorise a translation of the Bible into English. Edward VI's reign saw a marked swing towards Protestantism, and the *Book of Common Prayer* became the only authorised form of worship, the first edition in 1549, the second in 1552. In 1550 parishes were required to surrender their Latin worship books, as Worstead must have done, and to make an inventory of all their liturgical goods. In 1552-3 commissioners in each county went to every church to list the vessels and vestments it owned with the aid of the priest, the churchwardens and sometimes others - as in Worstead. The commissioners left a few essential items with the church but removed everything else, to be sold for the benefit of the crown. Many parishes, warned by the order to make an inventory in 1550, hid some items and sold others to fund repairs or relieve the poor, as was allowed.

Fig 55 The bells of St Mary's

In modernised English Worstead's short inventory of 1552 reads:

31 Aug. Thomas Blackburne clerk, vicar, William Taylor, John Short, parishioners, William Lenye, Thomas Valys, churchwardens.

In primis [first of all] *there are hanging in the steeple there 5 bells...* Their individual weights were estimated and their values calculated at 15s. per cwt or hundredweight (112 pounds or 55 kilos): the first bell of 3 cwt at 45s; the second of 5 cwt at £3.15s; the third of 8 cwt at £6; the fourth of 12 cwt at £9; the fifth of 16 cwt at £12. The bell clappers weighing 30 lb (pounds) were valued at 15s; the saunce [sanctus] bell at 5s; and three latten candle-sticks at 21d. Of these items the church was allowed to keep the fifth bell.

There then followed a copy of the inventory of 1550, with an introduction which implies that liturgical goods were removed in 1550, though this did not happen elsewhere in the Tunstead Hundred:

This is a true Copy of the Inventory that was taken by Sir Thomas Clere and Sir Thomas Woodhouse knights and Thomas Crooke Esquire and particular to the King's Majesty to the County of Norfolk Declaring all such goods pertaining to the said Church of Worstead and then Received by the said Sir Thomas Clere, Sir Thomas Woodhouse and Thomas Crooke by Virtue of a Letter from the King's Majesty's most honourable Council to them directed bearing the date the sixth day of August in the 4th year of the King's Majesty's reign [28.1.1550-27.1.1551] *that now is the tenor of which said inventory that do then appear here after following.*

Silver and plate:
In primis 2 crosses [one for processions, the other for visiting the sick]
2 basins [for ceremonial hand-washing]
2 candlesticks [parishioners providing lights before images used their own]
7 pairs of chalices [a chalice for the wine and a paten for the wafer bread]
2 pairs of censers [incense burners to 'cense' the altar, processions, etc]
2 pyxes [a 'silver' box to hang the reserved sacrament above the altar]
2 paxes [the pax was a small decorated disc with a handle kissed by the
          priest and congregation at the 'peace']
2 ships [a boat-shaped box for incense]
2 roddis [probably roods or crucifixes]
weighing in all by estimation with one chrismatory [for safeguarding the holy oils] *360 ounces.*

Item 2 copes [an outer cape worn by an officiating priest at mass and some other services] *of Baudkin cloth of gold* [silk interwoven with gold thread]
2 copes of blue velvet
2 copes of crimson velvet
2 copes of Damask [patterned silk]
one cope of black velvet
one cope of blue velvet
2 copes of silk (the one colour white, the other colour crimson)

2 copes of green silk
2 copes of Worsted colour black
2 [copes] of white fustian [a twilled linen fabric]
one vestment [usually the whole suit of vestments worn by a priest, deacon and subdeacon at mass] *of cloth of tissue* [a fine silk cloth interwoven with gold or silver thread] *with 2 tunicles* [worn by the subdeacon at mass] *of the same suit*
one vestment of blue velvet
one other vestment of blue velvet with tunicles to the same
one vestment of red velvet with 2 tunicles to the same
one vestment of white Damask with two tunicles to the same
one vestment of crimson velvet
one vestment of black velvet with 2 tunicles to the same
and one vestment of white silk with 2 tunicles to the same

Signed by Thomas Blackburn clerk [the vicar].

Fig 56 & 57 The Elizabethan Communion Table

There were enough chalices to serve the many altars in the medieval St Mary's, but too few of the other vessels and no altar frontals or coverings. The vestments listed are what one might expect for a large church with multiple altars, but no surplices are mentioned. The five tower bells were the norm for the Middle Ages, and the retention of the largest bell was usual. It is strange that no items other than the bell were noted as retained by the church: most churches were allowed to keep a chalice and paten, a surplice and two altar cloths. So the story of what happened in Worstead in 1552 is incomplete. However, somebody in the parish was strong enough to prevent any major damage to the images on the rood screens in Edward VI's reign (1547-53), except to the face of St Thomas of Canterbury, though the rood and the rood loft were removed. The stone altar in the northern chapel was torn out under Edward VI or Elizabeth I and the chapel's eastern wall still bears the scars. The Elizabethan communion table that now stands in its place would have been placed lengthways from east to west in the chancel for the celebration of the Last Supper.

3. The demise of St Andrew's Chapel

Fig 58 The site of St Andrew's Chapel

Richard Watts was buried in St Mary's south chapel in 1509 but left money for '*a priest to sing and pray six years in the church* [of St Mary] *except the Fryday in ev'ry week in the chapel of St Andrew's.*' His wife Agnes, buried in the same chapel in 1529, left money for the repair of St Andrew's and also gave meadow land to provide two lights in the church (St Mary's) for ever, '*if the king's law will permit.*' Did Agnes write this proviso or was it added by the vicar, who probably wrote the wills of his less literate parishioners? By 1529 Henry VIII's law suit seeking to annul his marriage to Catherine of Aragon was well under way and clergy were already uneasy about the implications of Henry's actions for the church. Whatever, Agnes would not have made her bequest to St Andrew's if she had thought it would soon close. So we may assume that the church was still active at least into the 1530s. In 1552-3 Edward VI's commissioners made inventories of every church's liturgical goods before confiscating them. An inventory exists for St Mary's (above), but the goods listed are hardly enough for the needs of St Mary's: there were none to spare for St Andrew's, for which no separate inventory survives. So St Andrew's became one of a hundred or so Norfolk churches that disappeared during the Reformation, probably not long before 1550.

Some of St Andrew's stones live on, because they were built into some sixteenth century buildings in Worstead, notably in the southern gable-end wall of Norwich House (*5* - NHER 30613) and in both gable-end walls of Bengate Farm (*23* - NHER 22716), though it is possible that some of the stone may have originated from the rebuilding of St Mary's chancel in the 1480s. The stone roof tiles that pave the rear yard of Norwich House may also have came from St Andrew's. Limestone is not found in Norfolk: it came from from Caen in Normandy or Barnack near Stamford, and was too expensive to be used in buildings other than churches and monasteries. Caen stone is smoother than Barnack, which is more fossil-filled: the stone in Worstead probably came by sea from Caen. Early Caen stone is whiter than the yellowy-buff limestone used in Victorian and later restorations. People who live close to the site of St Andrew's sometimes turn up pieces of limestone, some with carved ecclesiastical mouldings. Its site is now a green space between the top of St Andrew's Close and Swann's Yard. Unfortunately a geophysical survey of St Andrew's Field was unable to map the chapel's foundations, perhaps because a thick layer of rubble was dumped there when the Close was built in the 1970s.

Fig 59 Norwich House detail of south gable wall showing some ecclesiastical mouldings

4. Worstead's reluctance to change?

We do not know what happened in Worstead when Mary reintroduced the mass in 1553, but many people across Norfolk welcomed its return. Probably some of the necessary vestments and vessels came out of hiding or were bought back from those to whom they had been sold. Evidence from other places suggests that enough liturgical goods were found quite quickly, but that liturgical books were harder to find because most had been burned by the authorities.

When Elizabeth I reintroduced Protestantism and imposed the third edition of the *Book of Common Prayer* in 1559, there was little fuss, but the *Letterbook of John Parkhurst 1571-75* suggests that some people of Worstead, like many across Norfolk, were not enthusiastic. John Parkhurst, Bishop of Norwich 1560-75, an exile in Catholic Mary's reign, was the most evangelical of the bishops. He was ageing and badly served: his letters are often querulous and self-pitying, especially those to his erring collector of first fruits and tenths (clergy taxes), one George Thimelthorpe. George's brother Bertram lived in Worstead and was in trouble for his Catholic leanings during the Archbishop Matthew Parker's visitation of the Norwich Diocese in 1567, but he died in 1568. In 1571 Parkhurst sent Archbishop Parker a book he deemed heretical. It was written by Leonard Elson, Worstead's first named schoolmaster, although he was doubtless preceded by some chantry priests in the Middle Ages.

I signified to your Grace a yeare past of one Leonarde Elson, a scole master of Worsted - procured thither by Dr Gascon [the former Chancellor of the Diocese] - *who having written a fonnde* [?] *worke agaynst the state of true religion now used, and sending the same to a friend of his, I chaunsed* [chanced] *on the way to light uppon that boke. Which at that time I thought not meet to trouble your Grace withall, beyng in everye parte vnworthye the reading; so now, hearing hym to be apprehended and in the Gatehouse at Westminster, I thinke it not amysse together with theys lettres to send the same vnto your Grace, that having sufficiently wherewith to chardg hym, he may receive that to hym belongeth, and others by hys example warned to offend in the like.*

Your John Norvic

We do not hear the outcome of the case, but Parkhurst, a noted Calvinist, was more likely to complain of a closet Catholic than of an advocate of a more biblical church order.

In the same year Parkhurst enquired why there had been no communion at St Mary's on Whit Sunday. Late medieval Catholics took communion only once a year at Easter, but the new Church of England preferred three communions a year, and this became the rule in the Canons of 1604. In January 1575 Parkhurst also asked what had been done about the ringers of Worstead (and of St Faith's and Sprowston) who had rung for All Souls Night in 1574, a custom dear to religious conservatives but anathema to Puritans.

A curious incident occurred in 1588, the year of the Armada, when it was feared that Catholics might provide a fifth column for the threatened Spanish invasion. In the night of 6-7 August English fireships forced the Armada anchored off Gravelines to weigh anchor, and the wind drove the ships northwards, forcing them to circumnavigate Scotland to return home. Only seventy of the original 130 ships made it. In England the invasion scare continued, and the public celebration of victory was delayed until 24 November. In the meantime, on Friday 28 October, two Jesuit priests, Edward Oldcorne and John Gerrard, landed between Happisburgh and Bacton. Their aim was to reach London to reinforce the Jesuit mission in its efforts to reconvert England to Catholicism. The two separated, and John Gerrard, who in his true identity was known to the authorities as a committed Catholic, was detained under an alias in Worstead on Sunday 30 October. The officer of the watch was at worship in St Mary's and asked for the detainee to be brought to the church. Gerrard refused: it was deemed a sin for a Catholic to enter a church during a Protestant service. When questioned, his story that he was seeking a lost falcon seemed thin and the officer should have brought him before the Justice of the Peace. Instead he said that he had the look of an honest fellow and let him go (Gerrard was eventually captured in 1594, but escaped from the Tower in 1597). Did the officer suspect that his detainee was a Catholic, even a priest, and did he and others in Worstead have a lingering sympathy for Roman Catholicism, or at least for traditional worship?

5. Farming and the dissolution of the monasteries

The rise in England's population from some 3,160,000 to 4,110,000 during the reign of Elizabeth (1558-1603) stimulated the market for food. Growing demand and the increase in the size of landholdings for the survivors of the Black Death may together have accelerated the trend towards enclosure, whereby strips in the open fields were exchanged by agreement to make more compact and fenced holdings. Enclosure enabled go-ahead farmers to adopt new techniques without having to follow age-old communal practices. Worstead's earliest map is a copy made in 1781 by Robert Wymer from a late sixteenth century original probably drawn by Edmund Thurston. It names Worstead's open fields as *Mucklie, Broklie, Watch, Arplie* (Orpley, later Meeting House Hill), *Limbo, Bengate* and *Brigget*. This suggests that some of the hamlets in the parish had open fields of their own. Two more open fields were mentioned in sixteenth century documents, *Estgate* in 1527 and *Langley* in 1544. In the early Middle Ages these open fields probably covered as much as 62% of the parish, but the map shows that by the late sixteenth century they made up only 20-25%. The process of enclosure by agreement was gathering pace.

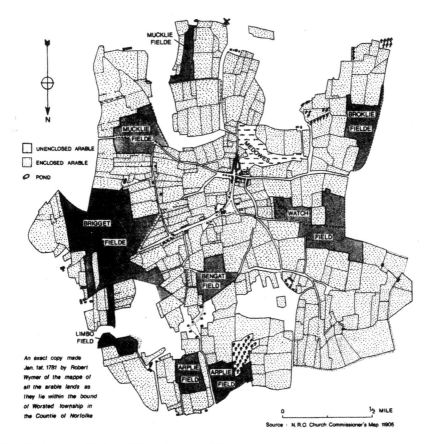

Fig 60 A copy of Robert Wymer's map of Worstead
Courtesy Norfolk Record Office Church Commissioner's Map 11905

After the dissolution of the monasteries in 1536-40 the new owners of former monastic lands in the parish probably welcomed the trend to enclosure. King Henry VIII had made the Bishop of Norwich exchange his diocesan revenues for those of St Benet's Abbey and of Hickling Priory: he profited by about £150 a year! St Benet's was not formally dissolved (though the last monk left in 1545) and its property in Worstead passed to the Bishop. In 1556-57 he farmed (leased) it for 41s.3d. a year to Bertram Themilthorpe. Other monastic lands in Worstead came into the ownership of the crown and then into private hands. In 1543-44 John Spencer of Norwich, already lord of the Worstead manor of Thruxtons (by then a manor was essentially a landholding with added customary rights and dues), bought the two Worstead manors formerly held by Pentney and Hempton Priories for £151.14s or about twenty times their annual value of £7.16s (what contemporaries called twenty years' purchase was the going rate for former monastic property). The manor once held by Bromholm Priory was granted on 26 May 1552 to Henry Grey, Duke of Suffolk, father of Lady Jane Grey, the ill-fated Nine Days' Queen. The Worstead lands formerly held by Ingham Priory probably passed to William Woodhouse. These changes in ownership may help to explain Worstead's complex manorial structure. Among the possessions of Sir George Berney Brograve in the early nineteenth century was the Manor of Worstead Hemptons, Pentons, Stapletons, Thruxtons, Wythes, and Heydons. Most names in the string can be tentatively identified: Hemptons as the former lands of Hempton Priory; Pentons perhaps as the former lands of Pentney Priory; Stapletons as the former lands of the Ingham estate in Worstead from the fourteenth century; Thruxtons as part of the Spencer estates in Worstead from before c.1270 to at least 1566 and maybe beyond; Wythes as the former lands of the Wythe family from the early fourteenth century to the early sixteenth; but Heydons as what? We need to know more.

Prosperity financed good farmhouses. Those of Worstead Hall Farm (*3* - NHER 22717) and of Lacey Farm (*33* - NHER 22715) began life in the sixteenth century, but underwent later alterations and additions. Bengate Farmhouse (*23* - NHER 22716) dates from the late sixteenth or early seventeenth century, though its original timber frame was gradually replaced in brick and flint between 1700 and 1820. Laurels Farmhouse belongs to a later date, but its barn dates from the seventeenth century (the village pound for stray animals that stood against its north wall vanished in its conversion in the early twenty-first century). The dwellings opposite the barn in Sloley Road may also have belonged to Laurels Farm. They appear to have been built on an earlier boundary wall which contains reused freestone, probably from St Andrew's, but the red brick diaper-work in the flint walls of the ground floor suggests a sixteenth or at the latest seventeenth century date. Another fine farmhouse of Tudor date was drawn by John Starling before it burned down in 1845. It lay in Withergate and was owned by Miles Baispoole in 1603/4. Baispoole family memorials appear in the floor of St Mary's and their names in the parish registers.

Fig 61 Sloley Road - The cottages opposite Laurels Farm Barn

6. Worstead's May Fair

There was, it seems, no medieval fair in Worstead, though neighbouring Sloley had a fair on St Bartholomew's Day (24 August), granted by royal charter to Oliver le Gros in 1334. Worstead Fair was granted to John Spencer by royal charter in Mary Tudor's reign (1553-58). The fair took place on the village green, or the Fairstead (*19*) as it was named in the Enclosure Award of 1827. The Fairstead then included the land on which the School (*20*) was built in 1845. The fair's main purpose was the buying and selling of livestock, particularly cattle and horses. The cattle were no doubt driven to and from the fair, most to Norwich but some perhaps to London. Other traders and entertainers will have paid a fee to the lord of the manor and set up stalls, many of them decorated with may blossom or hawthorn. Many sold things to eat, including the customary beans and bacon. Pedlars included fairs on their rounds, selling cheap trinkets, items of haberdashery (needles, ribbons, lace etc), and chapbooks (low cost booklets that included songs, jokes, short romances and religious writings, common until cheap newspapers arrived in the nineteenth century).

Fig 62 The Fairstead

7. Economic problems and the coming of the Strangers

The rebellion in Norfolk led by Robert Kett in 1549 did not involve Worstead but it was a symptom of the economic recession that afflicted the commerce of England and Norfolk during the Reformations of Henry VIII and Edward VI. Weavers had especial grievances as an act of 1555 stated:

The weavers of this realm have complained that the rich and wealthy clothiers do in many ways oppress them; some by setting up and keeping in their houses diverse looms, and keeping and maintaining them by journeymen and persons unskilful, to the decay of a great number of artificers which were brought up in the science of weaving...

Norwich weavers may have complained about the few Flemish weavers who settled in Norwich in the 1540s, but the arrival of more foreigners after 1565 revived the cloth trade. In 1564-65 a hard winter and a failed harvest left people hungry and trade in serious decline. '*Worsted making is greatly decayed*' wrote Mayor Thomas Sutherton of Norwich as he asked the Duke of Norfolk for help. The Duke obtained Letters Patent in November 1565 which allowed the Mayor to invite '*thirty Dutchmen of the Low Countries of Flanders*' (twenty-four were Dutch, six Walloons) together with their households (up to ten members) to settle in Norwich to make '*bays, arras, says, tapestry, mockadoes, stamens, carsey* (kersey?) *and such outlandish* [foreign] *commodities as hath not been used to be made within our realm of England.*' When in 1567 the Duke of Alva invaded the Low Countries and began to persecute Protestants, more refugees fled to England. Many of these Strangers settled in Norwich, where a list in March in 1571 recorded 3,925 foreigners, while a second list in October counted 4,013. Despite a serious outbreak of the plague in 1579-80 in which 4,193 Norwich citizens died, the Strangers numbered 4,677 by 1583, nearly a third of the city's population. The Strangers produced the *new draperies* or *stuffs* - luxury cloths that added new fibres like silk to worsted and used new finishing techniques. These cloths are described by Ursula Priestley (1990), but not all of them were new to Norfolk, for weavers were already making worsteds such as *stamens, camlets, says, satins* and *satin reverses*, and mixed cloths such as *bays, serges* and *dornix*. Cloth production in Norwich increased from 1193 lengths of cloth in 1566-67 to 34,097 by 1587-88. A document of 1575 says that the Strangers '*do not only set on work their own people, but also set on work our own people within the city, as also a great number of people near twenty miles about the city.*' That would include Worstead, though Worstead's weavers probably stuck to the plainer worsted cloths, because there are few references to worsted stuffs outside Norwich.

There are fewer evidences of wealth in Worstead's more 'urban' architecture in the later sixteenth century, although the north-south wing of Geoffrey the Dyer House (*3* - NHER 17024) on School Road shows diamond shapes picked out in blackened header bricks: such diaper work was common in Elizabethan England.

After 1536-40 the poor could no longer turn to the monastic almoner, and private charities were only slowly established. So the Elizabethan Poor Law of 1598 and 1601 (usually called the Old Poor Law) made the parish responsible for the relief of poverty. The Overseers of the Poor, elected by the parish vestry, had the power to raise a rate to relieve the old and sick in their own homes, apprentice pauper children, and send the able-bodied to houses of correction, if the parish had one following an act of 1576. Most parishes, including Worstead, could not afford to build one.

8. Protestant and Parliamentary Worstead?

By the time Elizabeth's reign ended in 1603 it seems that Worstead people were learning to accept Protestant beliefs and practices. In that year clergy were required to complete a return of how many communicants there were in their congregations: Vicar William Fleming reported quite a high figure of 296. Further small pieces of evidence suggest that Worstead was firmly Protestant during the turbulent seventeenth century. A memorial to James King, once in the floor, is now half-hidden in the wall behind the pulpit of St Mary's: '*Here resteth for a while till the dead shall rise the body of James King who decesed the XI daye of Maye Anno Dni 1617.*' He left £20. It bought three acres of land for the purpose of endowing sermons in St Mary's: strong Protestants set great store on sermons in the early seventeenth century (In 1836 the charity yielded £4.10s and spent £4 on four sermons, 5s. on the bell-ringers, and a mere 5s. on the poor). Thomas, son of Henry Pye, gentleman of Worstead, studied at Sir William Paston's Free School in North Walsham (founded in 1604/06) in 1621-24, went up to the notably Puritan Gonville and Caius College in Cambridge and was ordained. When Parliament went to war with the king in 1642, the gentry of the Tunstead Hundred were more Parliamentary and Puritan than Royalist and Anglican: it is likely that Thomas and his father Henry favoured the Roundheads, even if - like many in Norfolk - they were not involved in the fighting. By the time war broke out Worstead people had already shown little support for the policies of Charles I: the town was assessed at £22.7s. for Ship Money in 1634 but paid only 16s.

9. Farming in the Manor of Amners St Andrew in the Civil Wars

The Civil Wars and Interregnum of 1642-1660 brought changes in land ownership, when lands were confiscated by the victorious Parliament, or were sold to support the King in exile or to pay the fines imposed on active Royalists by Parliament. Parliament also confiscated the properties of bishops and cathedrals. So a survey of the Dean and Chapter properties in Norfolk was made in 1649. It included the Manor of Amners (Almoner's) St Andrew in Worstead. The Manor's demesne lands, some forty acres, were divided into eighteen small holdings: the largest was the fourteen acres of *Chappel Close* and the rest were all less than four acres. Some of these plots of land had names, such as *Bulls Close*, but most were defined by roads and by the boundaries of neighbouring plots. Four of the open fields were named: *Brocklie*, *Watch*, *Bengate* and *Mucklie*, sometimes with an added suffix confirming that part of the field had been enclosed by agreement among neighbours, as in *Watch Close* or *Mucklie Croft*. The annual value of the demesne lands and properties was assessed as £22.0s.4d. To this should be added the rents of assize (fixed customary rents) due from eleven free and twenty-seven copyhold tenants, worth £4.12s.0d; and other manorial receipts worth £1.2s.0d. Among the free tenants was Sir Charles le Grosse, probably a descendant of Oliver le Gros who founded the market and held manors in Sloley and Worstead. A striking feature of the survey is that the strips belonging to the Manor's demesne were not distributed evenly across the open fields: ten were concentrated in *Brocklie* and *Watch Field* (five each), with four more spread among *Bulls Close* (one), *Bengate Field* (one) and *Mucklie Field* (two). This confirms that enclosure by agreement was continuing.

Soon after this survey Manor Farm Barns, no doubt first built in timber or mud brick, probably began their rebuilding in Norfolk brick: some of their bricks have diagonal scintlings common in the later seventeenth century (scintlings or skintlings are the lines made on the face of a brick as it was placed for drying before being fired in the kiln).

10. Weaving and the cloth trade in Stuart Worstead

From the 1620s Norfolk suffered economic depression because trade was disrupted by an outbreak of the plague in 1625-26, by the Thirty Years War of 1618-48 and by the British Civil Wars of 1637-51. That the worsted and woollen industries remained in some difficulty is suggested by the Acts of 1667 and 1678 requiring the dead to be buried in shrouds made from wool. Blomefield records a tombstone in the chancel of St Mary's bearing a Latin inscription '*Hic lapis in pannis Spicer tenet osa Johannis*' or '*This stone holds the bones of John Spicer in wool*.' The acts were often ignored, but when in 1918 St Mary's churchyard was found to be full, some skeletons excavated were covered in remnants of woollen shrouds. Britain's trade strengthened in the later seventeenth century, and in 1697 Celia Fiennes wrote of Norwich that '*The textile industry employed men and women in spinning, weaving, dyeing, scouring, fulling or bleaching their stuffs*,' and added that the city '*looks like what it is, a rich, thriving industrious place*.' In and after 1685 many Huguenots, French Protestants, fled from the persecution of the Catholic King Louis XIV. Most settled in Spitalfields in London but some came to Norwich. Quite a number were silk weavers, and mixing silk and worsted gave Norwich another luxury cloth, crape. Some Huguenot names survive, such as Boileau, Columbine, Martineau, Noverre and Philippo: a Walter Philippo was farming in Worstead in 1912. We know of three worsted weavers active in Worstead in 1670-1700, when St Mary's baptismal register records the occupations of some of the parents who brought their children to be baptised:

Blacksmith: John Smith
Butcher: Thomas Lacy
Carpenters: Stephen More, Robert Smith
Cooper: John Hazelup
Grocer: John Car
Husbandmen (farmers): Robert and Thomas Thirtle
Labourers: Robert Buttrum, Robert Webster
Masons: Simon Butler, Richard Shalders
Miller: John Throry
Shoe-makers: John Austin, John Cook, Richard Smith
Tailors: John Martins, Charles Topcliff, John Watson
Thatcher: Philip Sadler.
Weavers: Edmund Hazelup, William Newstead, Thomas Smith

Figs 63 & 64 Interior of the workshop behind Norwich House.

The weavers of the seventeenth and early eighteenth century left more evidence in Worstead's buildings. The earliest is the weaver's cottage or workshop of c.1600 that stands behind Norwich House (*5* - NHER 30613). Its eaves were raised in the nineteenth century, but it still retains its cellar and internal divisions. Weaver's Cottage in Meeting Hill (*24* - NHER 16448) has a large weaver's window in its oldest part built in c.1650. Richard Culley lived there: he was the first Baptist minister in Meeting Hill from 1717, but earned his living as a weaver. John Starling drew a poorly constructed terrace of four weaver's cottages, which shared a kitchen, a privy and a well. Built after 1666 on the Front Street side of the former market square, they lost their roofs in a gale during World War II and were demolished. Lastly the east-west range of Geoffrey the Dyer's House (*3 -* NHER 17024) on Honing Row was probably formed from three weaver's cottages in the early eighteenth century: note the vertical dividing lines, the large window openings, and the reused knapped flints, perhaps from St Andrew's Church. Other cottages called weaver's cottages in postcards (White Cottage in Front Street) or on their gates (6 Honing Row, now renamed), probably do not deserve the title.

Fig 65 Geoffrey the Dyer House

That Worstead was still benefiting from worsted weaving, from the further expansion of towns and from the rapid growth of domestic and foreign trade in the late seventeenth and early eighteenth century is evident from the 'urban' buildings around Church Plain. The older buildings that made up the eastern range of the Manor House (*2 - NHER 17023*) had an expensive uplift soon after 1690, when a new facade was added with fine sash windows separated by a stylish platband between the storeys. This was paralleled on the east side of Church Plain in the Thatched House (*6 - NHER 17025*) and in St Andrew's Cottage above the Undercroft (*7 - NHER 19461*). The Thatched House shows two distinct building phases, with a second, later phase extending the front northwards by one bay and unifying the whole between Dutch gables. Though used earlier, Dutch gables became fashionable in East Anglia after the Glorious Revolution of 1688-89 which put the Protestant Dutch William of Orange and his English wife Mary on the throne. The facade of Norwich House (*5 - NHER 30613*) was renewed in the early to mid eighteenth century. After this burst of building on Church Plain, Worstead's Georgian splendour is almost entirely confined to farmhouses.

Fig 66 The Thatched House

11. Worstead and the Glorious Revolution of 1688-89

A Worstead man was close to the action in the Glorious Revolution. After the return of Charles II in 1660, the heir presumptive was his brother James, Duke of York. In 1673 James was exposed as a Roman Catholic and the Compton Census of 1676 was an attempt to gauge loyalty to the Church of England in the face of the probable Roman Catholic succession. The Census listed 351 Worstead people as conformist Anglicans, only ten as Protestant Nonconformists and none as Roman Catholics. When James succeeded his brother in 1685 he worked to give his co-religionists equal rights with Anglicans, who since the 1660s and 1670s were alone allowed to hold office under the crown. Protestants feared that James II intended to reconvert the country to Catholicism. Henry, son of Edmund Wharton, Vicar of Worstead, was born in 1664 with two tongues (I Rendall 2000) and was from the age of six in 1670/71 a pupil at the Paston School. Like Thomas Pye, he went up to Gonville and Caius College in Cambridge, was ordained and became a noted scholar. He served as chaplain to Archbishop William Sancroft of Canterbury, one of the famous Seven Bishops who defied James and triggered the Glorious Revolution of 1688-89. James fled and the crown was offered to the firm Protestants William of Orange and his wife Mary, daughter of James by his first wife. Henry died young in 1694/5, but left Worstead a lasting legacy. A board over St Mary's south door records the charity he established: *Rev Henry Wharton, chaplain to Archbishop Sancroft and son of Edward Wharton, vicar of this parish, did by will dated 1694 give the yearly rent of 22 acres at Shotesham after the deaths of his mother, father and sister, to the ornament of the church of Worstead as directed by the Trustees (the rectors of Westwick and Sloley, the vicars of Worstead and Honing).*

Fig 67   One of the many burial markers on the site of the first chapel behind Weaver's Cottage. The Trivett family were influential in the history of the settlement.

4. GEORGIAN WORSTEAD

1. The Baptists give Orpley a new name

The Baptists came to Orpley in 1717. The success of their settlement led to a change of name. As early as 1790 the Worstead Highways Book did not use the name Orpley but spoke of '… *carrying stones to the Meeting Beck…*'. Orpley was also ignored in the Enclosure Act 1821 and in the Award of 1827, and the first edition of the Ordnance Survey map of 1838 names the hamlet Meeting House Hill. This is still its official name. Orpley continued in erratic use on indentures of sale until 1860, but the last shows Ockley from a misreading of the 'r' and 'p' in an earlier document. Today the Royal Mail and the county's signage use Meeting Hill, the hamlet's name in almost all circumstances.

2. The antecedents of the Baptists of Meeting Hill

The origins of the Baptists in North Norfolk take us back into the seventeenth century. Christians who rejected infant baptism and insisted on adult believer's baptism emerged during the Reformations of the sixteenth century. In England they were found among the Puritans who formed churches for believers who felt themselves to be among the 'elect' - those according to Calvinist theology who were predestined by God to eternal salvation. Puritans were persecuted under Elizabeth I, James I and Charles I. Some emigrated to America, notably the Mayflower Pilgrims in 1620, but more moved to Holland, where English churches were formed in several Dutch towns, one in Rotterdam as early as 1611. Some fled from Great Yarmouth and Norwich in the 1630s when Matthew Wren was Bishop of Norwich. Wren, like Archbishop William Laud of Canterbury, tried to impose more Catholic (but not Roman Catholic) forms of worship and was strongly opposed to the Calvinist theology favoured by Puritans. Many exiles returned when the Long Parliament, elected in 1640, began to limit the powers of King Charles I and then went to war against him in 1642. Some returnees planted a church in Great Yarmouth in 1642 and a sister church in Norwich in 1644. The two churches helped to found similar churches across Norfolk and some of them adopted Baptist beliefs as early as 1646.

When the monarchy was restored in 1660 the Church of England returned with Charles II. In 1662 the Act of Uniformity required all worshippers to follow the *Book of Common Prayer* (the fifth edition), and the Conventicles Act of 1664 penalised all who worshipped in other ways. The act lapsed after three years and in 1669 every bishop was required to list any conventicles in his diocese. Bishop Edwards Reynolds of Norwich, a former Presbyterian, made his return to Archbishop Gilbert Sheldon, listing three conventicles in North Walsham ('*one of Quakers, another of Saturday observers, a third of Independents*') and others at Bradfield, East Ruston, Trunch and Tunstead. All of them existed before 1660. Richard Breviter, Vicar of North Walsham from 1651, formed an Independent church there in 1652. In 1656 he adopted Baptist beliefs and baptised many of his adult congregation, many of whom became 'Seventh Day' Baptists (probably the '*Saturday observers*' listed by Reynolds in 1669). Those who disagreed with these Baptists formed a second church in a barn in Bradfield. In 1669 the Bradfield church was associated with one at Tunstead, formed in 1652 and led by John Green, who became Vicar of Tunstead in 1657, only to be ejected in 1660.

In 1670 a second Conventicles Act punished all worship outside the Church of England, but in 1672-73 Charles II's Declaration of Indulgence gave Dissenters freedom to worship publicly in premises licensed by the authorities. John Green was licensed at Dilham and Tunstead. Other Baptists were licensed near Meeting Hill: Henry Symonds at John Hagge's house in North Walsham, John Woolston at Samuel Durrant's house in Ingham, and Robert Wood at Elizabeth Becker's house in East Ruston. After the Glorious Revolution of 1688-89 the Toleration Act gave freedom of worship in licensed meeting places to 'safe' Dissenters. Soon Particular Baptist churches (those embracing a Calvinist theology) were licensed at Ingham, Norwich, Pulham and Great Ellingham. Thomas Grantham from Lincolnshire started General Baptist churches (those critical of Calvinism) in Norwich in 1686, in Kings Lynn and Great Yarmouth in 1689, and in Smallburgh in 1691. The General Baptists of Smallburgh existed in an area where most Baptists had been Calvinists since the 1650s.

3. The growth of the Baptist settlement

In 1717 Richard Culley led a group from Smallburgh to establish a Particular (Calvinistic) Baptist church in the hamlet of Orpley in the parish of Worstead. On 4 December 1717 the church began to worship in a barn behind the present Weaver's Cottage *(24,-* NHER *16448).* Richard Culley was chosen *'as Elder over the Church'* on the same day, when five deacons were also appointed. The office of deacon was regarded as so important that candidates were often put on probation (John Groom, Luke Manning and John Gunnell served their probation from June 1735 to May 1738). The list of 'original members' who established the new church contains 120 names, but the list includes new admissions down to 1740. So those who left Smallburgh may have been fewer in number, perhaps as few as thirty or forty. However, if another list of thirty-four male names in the earliest church register records founding members, then the number may be somewhat greater, for there would surely have been women among them. The separation seems to have been amicable, for as late as 1733 a church meeting of Worstead Baptist Church was held at Smallburgh: it expelled Thomas Wright of Horning because he broke the Sabbath by working and by frequenting public houses.

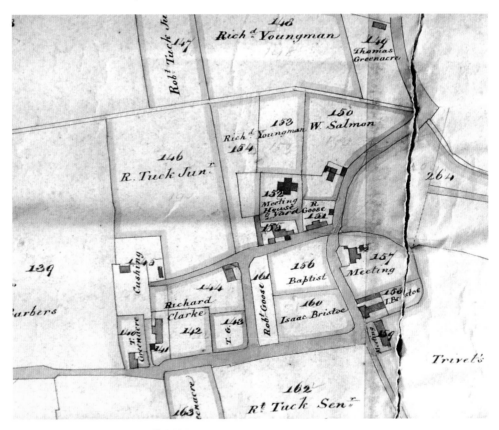

Fig 68 Map of Meeting Hill 1825
Courtesy Norfolk Record Office, Norcat ref. BR276/1/1118

Richard Culley died in 1729 and is said to have been '*succeeded*' by his son Titus. What '*succeeded*' meant is not entirely clear and it may be that Thomas Bennett was the next pastor. He was received into membership in 1732 and then signed the minutes of church meetings, but he is not mentioned after November 1734. The next certain pastor was Edward Trivett. He was born in 1712 and was baptised in Meeting Hill at the age of 25. His ministry probably began early in 1742, but he may have been on probation before then. He baptised Mary Watts on 24 July 1742, '*the first time I was ever employed in such work. May God bless my poor labours and small beginning with abundant success to the glory of His own Name.*' His ministry of fifty years ended with his death in 1792. Edward Trivett trained a dozen ministers, wrote worthy hymns, penned a book *Baptists vindicated from some groundless and false charges* in 1770, and baptised 391 people, many of them in the river or the little stream that ran beside the chapel. The last of his seven children, Zenas Trivett, minster at Langham in Essex in 1778-1819, returned to Norfolk and died in 1831, when the church register describes him as '*the last of the Sabbatarians at Worstead.*' How Worstead Baptist Church was connected with the Seventh Day Baptists (see section 2 above) is unclear, but Edward Trivett's successor, James Freeman Beard, came to Meeting Hill from a Seventh-Day Baptist church in Woodbridge.

A record has survived from 1791 noting the quarterly '*subscriptions*' made by each of forty-four members. The most frequent payment was a shilling but other amounts paid appear in brackets after the name in the list:

Thomas Abigail (5s.)	Benjamin Helsdon (2s.6d)
Harr [Harry or Harriet?] August	[?] Harris (2s.)
John Barcham (15s.)	William Love (5s.)
William Barton (2s.)	Elizabeth Maris (1s.6d.)
Mrs Baldwin	Thomas Nobbs (2s.6d.)
Conc [?] Black (1s.6d.)	Jacob Palmer (5s.)
Richard Culley (15s.)	John Palmer (1s.6d.)
Robert Cook (3s.)	Charles Plummer
Thomas Cooper	[? Widow] Riches (2s.6d.)
[?] Chase	[?] Ramsdale,
Thomas Dawson	[?] Shalders senior
John Delf (2s.)	[?] Shalders junior (2s.)

William Drake	[?] Simpson senior (3s.),
Samuel Dunham	[?] Simpson junior (5s.)
Mrs Fiddy (2s.6d.)	Mrs [?] Saul (5s.3d.)
William Goose	Robert Tuck (5s.)
Jonathan Harris (2s.6d.)	Han[nah?] Temple,
Josiah Harmer (2s.)	Mrs [?] Temple,
Harbert senior	James Trivett
Harbert junior	[?] Thickson [a dubious reading]
Mrs Hannant (5s.)	[?] Tompson
John Howes	Sarah Wigg (2s.6d.).

There were surely more members than forty-four, because there were 188 in 1798. The non-payment of subscriptions seem to have been a grumbling issue over the years, as a resolution of a Church Meeting on 26 May 1850 still in the *Manual* of 1898 implies:

That, as several members of the Church do not subscribe to the support of the Gospel, it be impressed upon the mind of every member that it is the duty and privilege to contribute to that object, it being quite evident that membership involves responsibilities of the kind.

An idea of the geographical spread of those who worshipped in Meeting Hill is suggested by the births registered in one year:

Marseah, daughter of John & Hannah Beane, at Sutton on 16.4.1791
Sarah, daughter of Robert & Hannah Shackle, at Dilham on 17.4.1791
Phillis, daughter of Thomas & Mary Nobbs, at Ridlington on 24.4.1791
Elouisa, daughter of Nehemiah & Phillis Trivett, at Walsham on 8.7.1791
John, son of William and Hannah Goose, on 3.11.1791
Hannah, daughter of William & Hannah Riches, at Honing on 2512.1791
Rhoda, daughter of William & Ann Bertent [?], at Lammas on 29.12.1791

James Freeman Beard was ordained pastor in 1794 in quite an elaborate ceremony:

The worship of God began at 10 o'clock in the morning with singing the 2nd part of the 84th Psalm of Dr Watts's, after which Bro.[Charles] Farmery of Diss engaged in prayer earnestly imploring a blessing on the important

work of the day. Brother Ridley of Ipswich introduced the work of the day
and interrogated the parties particularly interested therein, agreeable to
which Brother Shalders, the Senior Deacon, stood up and gave a brief
account [of the steps] the church had taken in her widowhood state, of
the particular providences occurring in bringing J.F. Beard among them
and their unanimous approbation of him. Then J.F. Beard rose and gave a
brief account relative to his call by grace, his call to the ministry and the
leading of Providence in his removal from Woodbridge to Worstead, etc,
which being done he gave a confession of faith to the glorious doctrines
of the everlasting gospel. The Senior Deacon in the name of the church
recognized their call and J.F. Beard his acceptation of the pastoral office
among them, at the conclusion of which [was] sung [the] 132nd Psalm
[in] Dr Watts Long Measure. After which Brother Hitchcock of Wattisham
gave the charge from 1 Timothy 4.16. [Then was] sung [the] 103rd Psalm
[from] the first book [of] Dr Watts and Brother Brown of Yarmouth
addressed the church from Eph[esians] 2.19. Then was sung the 132nd
Psalm from the pause [in?] Dr Watts's Book, and Brother Kinghorn of
Norwich concluded in prayer.

Of those mentioned in this description, Brother Farmery of Diss had himself been
ordained by Edward Trivett. Brother Shalders was no doubt one of the Shalders
family who owned so much property in Worstead's village centre, probably Jacob
who died around 1800. Brother Joseph Kinghorn was the influential pastor of
St Mary's Particular Baptist Church in Norwich, who trained John Rix Blakely,
the pastor in Meeting Hill in 1832/3-37. James Beard, the new minister, was
keen to tackle lapsed members and visitors were sent to question Robert Tuck of
Worstead, Brother Thompson of Stalham, John Marjoram of Felmingham and
Brother Blackbone of Horstead. As a result of further visiting James Hannant was
readmitted to membership in 1796. James Beard's ministry was fruitful: he had
baptised 130 people by 1811, when he left for Ipswich.

4. Worsted weaving and the Industrial Revolution

As Richard Culley worked as a weaver and as the Baptist pastor, Daniel
Defoe published his *Tour through the Eastern Counties* (1724), the first
instalment of his *Tour Through the Whole Island of Great Britain*. In it he
underlined the success of Norfolk's worsted industry:

When we come into Norfolk we see a face of diligence spread across the whole county; the vast manufactures, carried on (in chief) by the Norwich weavers, employs all the country round in spinning yarn for them; besides many thousands of packs of yarn which they receive from other countries [counties]*, even from as far as Yorkshire and Westmoreland.*

He goes on to mention '*several good market towns, and innumerable villages, all diligently applying to the woollen [worsted] manufacture.*' He identifies Worstead as one of those towns, alongside Aylsham, Cawston, Holt, North Walsham and Reepham. It all looked good: 6,000 Norwich looms in 1700 became 12,000 in 1770, needing 72,000 to 96,000 hand spinners to keep them working. Yet even as it expanded Norfolk's worsted industry encountered competition, first of all from Indian cottons, known as calicos, and then from the growing worsted industry in Yorkshire.

Cotton was a lighter, more easily washed fabric than worsted, and its yarn was strong enough to cope with such early machines as Kay's Flying Shuttle of 1733, Hargreaves' Spinning Jenny of 1767, Arkright's Water Frame of 1769, Crompton's Spinning Mule of 1779, and Cartwright's Power Loom of 1785. Parliament heard the pleas of protesting weavers and passed acts in 1700 and 1721 to protect the worsted and woollen industries by banning the sale, use and wearing of calicos on pain of a fine. However the Lancashire-based cotton industry was strong enough to secure the repeal of the 1721 Act in 1773. Then the movement towards free trade swept away all the legislative protection for worsted manufacture by 1809 and created open markets in raw materials and cloth by 1824.

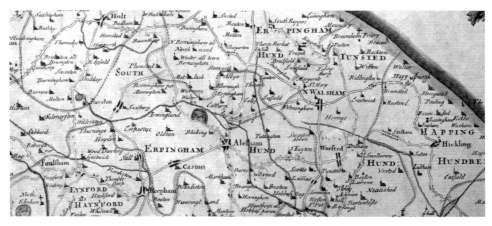

Fig 69 Extract from Robert Morden's Map 1695. Note Defoe's Market Towns: Holt, Reepham, Ca(w)ston, A(y)lesham, Wursted, N Walsham.

89

More serious was the competition of worsteds of lower and middle quality made in the West Riding of Yorkshire from the late seventeenth century. By 1772 the output of the West Riding equalled that of Norfolk. Machines invented for cotton were adapted to spin worsted yarn: the Spinning Jenny in 1794 and the Water Frame from c.1810. The first machine-spun worsted yarn arrived from Yorkshire in 1810 and within a decade most Norfolk weavers were using it. Stronger yarn meant that Cartwright's power loom was adopted in Yorkshire as early as the 1790s, and Norfolk's worsted industry was quickly overtaken.

So, even as the Norfolk worsted industry reached its greatest capacity, there were serious problems. John Wesley, visiting Norwich in October 1772, noted in his *Journal*:

Finding an abundance of people out of work, and consequently in the utmost want (such a general decay of trade having hardly been known in the memory of man), I enforced [stressed] *in the evening, 'Seek ye first the kingdom of God, and his righteousness; and all these things shall be added unto you.*

On 11 January 1781 the Reverend James Woodforde noted in his diary: '*Trade at Norwich never worse. Poor no employment.*' As he wrote the American War of Independence (1774-83) had begun a serious disruption of trade that was intensified by the French Wars (1792-1815). Norfolk's worsted industry never recovered. Norwich stuffs were luxury goods, vulnerable to the changing whims of fashion and to undercutting by cheaper, machine-made imitations. Worstead's plainer worsteds were better made by machine in Yorkshire, which had easy access to water and then steam power to drive its machinery. Norfolk was too slow to apply the new technology: no spinning mill opened in Norwich until the Albion Mills in 1836; no weaving mill until the St James and St Edmunds Mills in 1839. By 1856 Britain had 38,956 power looms: Norfolk had 428. Hand-loom weavers could no longer earn a living wage: in 1840 a government commission reported that a hand-loom weaver earned 6s or 7s a week in Yorkshire, but less elsewhere, well below a Norfolk farmworker's poor wage of 10s or 11s.

White's Directory of Norfolk of 1836, writing about Worstead, says '*This manufacture [worsted] left its ancient seat in Norfolk many years ago and is now chiefly confined to Norwich and its neighbourhood.*' The Poor Law Commission of 1834 reported a little part-time weaving in Worstead but found little employment outside farming in the rural parishes north of Norwich. The decline of worsted weaving had probably begun earlier in these country parishes than in the city, because after 1730 there was a rapid fall in the number of weavers outside Norwich taking out Sun Insurance policies. Weavers were mentioned in the parish registers in the early nineteenth century:

Samuel Cole six times between 1813 and 1829
Richard Appleton 1824 (he was a labourer in 1827 and a butcher in 1829)
Robert Appleton 1825
James Pointer 1825 (he was a labourer by 1827)
John Pycroft 1825.

No one appears as a weaver in the parish records after 1829. Worstead's last weaver is said to have been John Cubitt, the son of a master weaver who had owned three looms. John lived in Lyngate and is recorded as a farm labourer in the parish registers when six of his children were born between 1817 and 1828, and again in the censuses of 1861 and 1871. He was probably a farm labourer for most of his working life and perhaps a part-time weaver in the early part of it. He died, it is said, in 1882 in the Smallburgh House of Industry (the workhouse), but the 1881 census does not show him among the inmates. He was then reputedly 90 or 91 years of age: the census makes him 45 in 1841, 70 in 1861, 77 in 1871!

5. Worstead's public houses

The story runs that in the early nineteenth century the worsted cloth went to be sold in Norwich on a Saturday. The agent returned on Sunday to pay the weavers, whose celebrations in the pub close to the east end of the church, probably the Sign of the Lemon, disturbed the church services. The weavers were probably not guilty, for there was only a little part-time weaving left by the 1820s and 1830s. Even so, in 1825 Sir George Berney Brograve remodelled an earlier (seventeenth century?) house to create the New Inn (*15 - NHER 47221*), giving it a late Georgian frontage. Its cellars are not on the same alignment and were probably those of an earlier building. The first recorded licensee was John Rowland, described as a '*porter merchant and victualler.*' He held the inn in 1830-51 and appears in the 1851 census as a farmer of 31 acres. The New Inn was renamed the White Lady in 2011 on the basis of an unlikely story of a ghost of a lady in white who reputedly appears at midnight on Christmas Eve in St Mary's. In 1830 a man was drinking in the King's Head and boasted that he was not afraid of the White Lady: he would ring in the birth of Christ, as was Worstead's custom. He climbed into the ringing chamber, saying that, if he met the White Lady, he would give her a kiss. When he did not return, friends went to the church and found him huddled in terror. He whispered 'I've seen her' and died. Publicity about the new name in 2011 led Mrs Diane Bertholet to bring forward a photograph taken on 2 August 1975: it seems to show a ghostly figure behind Mrs Bertholet as she sat on a bench in St Mary's (see the *North Norfolk News* of 28 July 2011).

Fig 70 The Kings Head up to 1970 now Church View House

Since the late eighteenth century there are records of three other named public houses in the parish of Worstead. The King's Head, now Church View House (*18*) was leased by a Mr Hart from Mr Brograve in 1774 and sold beer supplied by William Hardy. Its earliest recorded licensee was Robert Watts in 1788. It closed in 1970. The White Swan seems to have had a short existence: it was licensed briefly to William Whall in 1793, 1794 and 1797. The first recorded licence of the White Horse (*28*) in Briggate was issued to James Willomont in 1794. It closed in 1957.

6. Worstead in Norfolk's Agricultural Revolution

  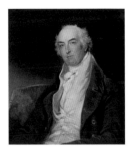

Fig 71 Richard Weston   *Fig 72 Charles Townshend*   *Fig 73 Thomas William Coke*
1591-1672   *1674-1738*   *1752-1842*

As early as 1722 Daniel Defoe noted that '*the country is exceedingly fruitful and fertile as well in corn as in pastures.*' And between 1720 and 1840 Norfolk led the Agrarian Revolution. The famous names are Charles, Viscount 'Turnip' Townshend of Raynham (1674-1738); Thomas William Coke of Holkham (1752-1842), created Earl of Leicester in 1834; and journalist Arthur Young, renowned for his *General View of the Agriculture of the County of Norfolk* of 1804. Townshend, Coke and other landlords certainly encouraged best practice: they wanted yields to rise without exhausting the soil, so that they could increase rents. However they all depended greatly on earlier work: a predecessor of Thomas Coke had already raised the rental value of the Holkham Estate by 44% between 1718 and 1758. And it took less well-known, experimental farmers to apply the new techniques of the Agrarian Revolution across the county.

Some of Norfolk's land needed improvement but Worstead's fertile loams needed little, though some needed drainage, at first by brushwood or furze-filled drains, perhaps from the 1830s by a mole plough, and finally by pottery drains. Marl, a mixture of clay and chalk/lime added to light soils to improve the texture, was not needed in Worstead, unless the sandy subsoil outcropped on the surface. Farmers had long used animal dung to fertilise the soil. Oilcake, a by-product of rape and linseed oil extraction, was introduced as a fertiliser in the 1770s, but was more often fed to livestock to improve their dung.

The biggest improvement in the quality and efficient usage of land was the introduction into crop rotations of turnips and clover from Holland by Sir Richard Weston (1591-1672). So the famed Norfolk Four Course Rotation predated 'Turnip' Townshend, who publicised it from 1730. The rotation over four years of turnips, barley, clover and wheat eliminated the need for fields to lie fallow one year in three, a big saving because fallow land had to be ploughed several times before barley or wheat could be sown. If turnips, grown as a fodder crop, were planted in rows, hoeing the weeds between them twice a year was easy and cleansed the soil. Clover fixed nitrogen in the soil and provided a fodder crop. Crops became more varied in the nineteenth century: rye and oats might be added; peas, beans or artificial grasses might replace clover; and mangold wurzels were often preferred to turnips for their greater resistance to disease. Longer rotations were tried - with some success when combined with artificial fertilisers - but all rotations aimed to increase yields. Yields varied a great deal, but a typical yield was 1:5 in the fourteenth century (plant one seed and get five back, but keep one to plant next year); 1:7 in the seventeenth, 1:10 in the nineteenth; 1:15 in the mid twentieth; and 1:30 or more now. Increasing yields enabled farmers to feed a population of England and Wales that rose from 9,000,000 to 18,000,000 in 1801-51 and became increasingly urban.

Norfolk also enclosed its open fields, parcelling out land in more compact units or farms. Enclosure, by agreement or statute, let farmers and landowners experiment and introduce new methods, especially if landlords let out land on long leases and in larger units. Farms grew in size, but probably not by much in fertile north-east Norfolk, where in 1851 40% of farms were still under fifty acres. As we have seen, early enclosures were made piecemeal by agreement between owners, and some of these were regularised in the Worstead Enclosure Act of 1821 and in the Enclosure Award of 1827. Where there was no dominant landowner, enclosure by act of Parliament was the norm after 1815, as in Worstead. Worstead's open fields then covered less than 15% of the land and the main reason to seek the Act of 1821 was to enclose the commons: the Award of 1827 enclosed 309 acres of common, waste and heath. Few of Worstead's early field boundaries survived the Enclosure Award: those that did are usually curved, not straight like those laid out in 1827.

The Award created the conditions for more productive farming, but the process favoured the rich landowners. In the early eighteenth century the major landowner in Westwick and Worstead had been John Berney. He had no sons and so he left most of his Worstead lands to the son of his elder daughter Julian (or Juliana) and Thomas Brograve, provided that the son took the surname Berney. After his mother died in 1768, Berney Brograve Berney evicted his tenants and farmed his estate himself. In 1773 he demolished the old Hall (called Muckley Hall from the sixteenth century, its clock survives in North Walsham's Market Cross). The architect James Wyatt (1746-1813) designed the new Worstead House (*38* - NHER 15440), which was built south of the old Hall quite possibly as early as 1768-74, as Cheryl Nicol (2015) argues. It is said that Humphrey Repton (1752-1818) landscaped the park of 300 acres and its large lake, but hard evidence is lacking: the park only reached its full size in 1844, aided by the enclosure of a key piece of common land in 1827. The Award shows that in 1827 Sir George Berney Brograve (the eccentric son of Berney Brograve Berney) owned the southern third of the parish together with Bengate Farm. He died childless in 1828 and the Estate was sold to the Hon. William Rufus Rous (1796-1875), third son of the first Earl of Stradbroke (the Stradbroke estate is still at Henham, Suffolk). *White's Directory of 1836* names Rous as a major landowner in Worstead alongside Jack Petre of Westwick House and John Postle of Holly House, Smallburgh. Jack Petre was the son of John Berney's younger daughter Elizabeth and William Petre: Jack inherited the Westwick Estate including lands in Worstead. The Tithe Apportionment of 1844 shows that John Postle owned much of the central part of the parish.

A poll book records the names of those from the parish who voted in the 1833 election for the two Knights of the Shire for Norfolk:

William Banyer,	John Goose
John Barnard	John Lacey (O)
William Blackburn	William Nash (O)
Rev John Blakeley	Thomas Nelson
Matthew Clarke	Robert Ostler (O)
Peter Clarke	William Postle,
Rev Richard Clarke (copyholder, hereafter C)	Hon William Rufus Rous
William Cook (occupier, hereafter O)	James Tooley (C)
John Cross	Robert Tuck
Samuel Cushion	Joseph Tuck
Edward Dyball (C)	Miles Wiseman
Benjamin Gibson (O)	James Wright.
Thomas Greenacre	

To qualify to vote in the county election after the Great Reform Bill of 1832 you needed to own freehold property worth at least forty shillings (£2) a year; to be a copyholder of land worth at least £10 a year; or to be an occupier of rented or leased land worth at least £50 a year. The large landowners appeared on this poll list (Jack Petre appeared on Westwick's list), but some of the occupiers were substantial tenant farmers. Some on the list were smaller freeholders, not wealthy enough to be named in *White's Directory* of 1836.

Small landowners often could not afford to hedge or fence their plots and many sold up, becoming landless labourers in an over-crowded labour market. They also lost their grazing rights on Worstead's former common land. A contemporary jingle is often quoted:

The law locks up the man or woman
Who steals the goose from off the common,
But leaves the greater villain loose
Who steals the common from the goose.

Up to the eighteenth century worsted weaving helped farming by creating employment in winter when there was less work on the farms; and farming helped worsted manufacture by providing casual employment when full-time weavers were short of work. The migration of worsted manufacture to Yorkshire from the mid eighteenth century then created the pool of cheap labour on which Norfolk's agrarian revolution depended.

Cattle and sheep were important in Norfolk agriculture, though there were probably more cattle than sheep in Worstead. In times when cereal prices crashed - in the 1780s, 1820s and 1880s - agrarian prosperity was rebuilt on livestock farming. Worstead's May Fair was noted for its fat bullocks, according to William Marshall's *Rural Economy of Norfolk* of 1787. In that year there were no more than a hundred, but only twenty of them fat, but there were some 300 head of cattle, mostly two year-olds. Most of the livestock was sold to Norwich butchers. The fair was held on May Day until 1752, when Britain replaced its Julian calendar with Europe's more accurate Gregorian calendar: eleven days (3 to 13 September 1752) were omitted and the calendar jumped from 2 to 14 September. To make up for the lost days many communities moved events on by 11 days: Worstead Fair moved to Old May Day or 12 May. Sometime after 1836 a second day (13 May) was added.

The rotation of crops supported livestock throughout the year - formerly most livestock was slaughtered and salted at Martinmas (11 November). Turnip tops were grazed in the field before the roots were lifted, chopped and fed with chaff to cattle in yards as they stood on straw litter. The litter was then used to manure the fields. Growing clover or artificial grasses allowed animals to graze and manure the land at the same time. Norfolk was involved in selective breeding, pioneered by Robert Bakewell in Leicestershire and promoted by Coke at his 'sheep shearings' at Holkham in the early nineteenth century: in the eighteenth century the average weight of sheep sold at Smithfield almost tripled and the average weight of cattle more than doubled. However many Norfolk farmers preferred half-breeds to the pedigree New Leicester or Southdown sheep.

Norfolk adopted some of the new machines, but rather slowly. The all-iron, wheeled plough, produced by Ransome's in 1808, became common from the 1820s, drawn by shire horses improved by selective breeding. Jethro Tull's seed drill of 1701 and his *Horse-Hoeing Husbandry* of 1733, both promoted by Townshend, could have eased weeding between drilled rows of seed, but cheap labour planted seeds with dibbers/dibblers and weeded with hand-wielded hoes: the hoe was arguably the most used Norfolk tool well into the nineteenth century. The scythe replaced the medieval sickle in the early nineteenth century, when the cradle was attached, because it left longer straw and was quicker. The static and horse-powered threshing machine, invented by Andrew Meikle in 1786, was rare in Norfolk until the late 1820s and not very common thereafter.

7. Ups and downs in farming from the 1790s to the 1840s

As the Agrarian Revolution progressed, farmers profited from high corn prices in the French Wars of 1792-1815 and many improved their farms with new buildings. Manor Farm's brick barns were probably expanded during these Wars. The Georgian Laurels Farmhouse (*13* - NHER 52509) was built in white brick (made from lime-rich clay and usually grey or buff in colour) and roofed in slate, which were both quite rare materials before the railway reached Worstead in 1874. A Georgian frontage was added to Holly Grove House *(21)*, and Lyngate House *(22)* was built, probably as the residence of a gentleman-farmer. Perhaps some of the good estate cottages, built by the eccentric Sir George Berney Brograve should be included in this phase, notably New Lane Cottage (*34* - NHER 47222*) and Swan Cottage, built in 1824 (*29* - NHER 47795).

A cycle of booms and slumps afflicted the economy from 1816 to the 1840s. Farmers were helped by the Corn Laws of 1816 which - despite modifications in 1822 and 1828 - kept prices artificially high until their repeal in 1846. Farm labourers suffered from the high price of bread, their staple food, and from wages kept low by the lack of other jobs. William Marshall wrote in 1787: '*A Norfolk labourer will do as much for one shilling as two men in many other places will do for eighteen pence each.*' Nathaniel Kent in his *General View of the Agriculture of Norfolk* of 1796 recorded that since 1750 prices had risen by 60% but wages by only 25%. So real wages - what money wages will buy - had fallen considerably. As the Poor Law Commission found in 1834, farm labour was the main employment in north Norfolk, and much of it was piece-work (such as hoeing, sowing, threshing, ditching, hedging or draining). This was offered to the pool of casual labourers: calculations from the censuses of 1831 and 1841 suggest there were three casuals to every two full-timers; while other figures suggest one man in eight was unemployed. Full-time employees who had once lived in (especially the skilled horsemen, ploughmen, cowmen and shepherds) were from the 1790s offered a cottage or an allowance, which left them more vulnerable to price rises. There was real hunger.

Fig 74 Laurels Farmhouse

Across East Anglia farm labourers rioted, demanding higher wages, in 1816, 1822, 1830-31, 1835-37 and 1843-44. In the Swing Riots of 1830-31 labourers set fire to ricks and threshing machines which, they said, took away their winter work of hand-threshing by flail. Disturbances occurred in more than 150 Norfolk parishes, one at a wage meeting in Worstead. On 24 November 1830 the JPs of the Tunstead and Happing Hundreds issued a statement at North Walsham:

It is their opinion that such disturbances principally arise from the use of Threshing machines, and [from] the insufficient Wages of the Labourers. The Magistrates therefore beg to recommend to the Owners and Occupiers of Land in these Hundreds to discontinue the use of Threshing Machines, and to increase the Wages of Labour to Ten Shillings a week for able-bodied men, and that when task work is preferred, that it should be put out at such a rate as to enable an industrious man to earn Two Shillings per day.

Few threshing machines existed in the locality, but even as late as the 1840s some farm workers in north-east Norfolk were still paid as little as 8s. or 9s. a week with a harvest wage of £5 or £6. One of the sad effects of the agrarian protests was the decline of trust between masters and men, and the lack of charity offered by the former to the latter.

Many resented the enforced payment of tithes to support the Anglican Rector or Vicar: compulsion to give a tenth of one's produce to the church began in the eighth century. In Worstead the Rector was the Dean and Chapter of Norwich Cathedral, who took the great tithe on corn and left the lesser tithes to the Vicar. Dissenters objected to paying tithes to a priest whose services they did not use. Farmers, hard-pressed in the years after 1815, saw a tenth of their produce going to a priest whose lot was not so hard as theirs. And farm workers objected that they were more entitled to fair wages from the farmers' profits than the vicar living in his fine vicarage. In 1836 the Tithe Commutation Act turned the tithe into a rent charge based on the price of corn and spread among the owners of land liable to the tithe. Some 63% of parishes accepted the rent charge, but the apportioning of the tithe among the parishes took some years. The matter was settled in Worstead by the Tithe Apportionment of 1844, but even then some farmers failed to see why the Vicar of Worstead should have a steady income of £270 a year when their income fluctuated. Grumbles about tithes continued until their last vestiges disappeared in 1951.

8. The relief of poverty

Ill fares the land, to hast'ning ills a prey,
Where wealth accumulates, and men decay;

Prices and lords may flourish, or may fade;
A breath can make them, as a breath has made;
But a bold peasantry, their country's pride,
When once destroyed, can never be supplied.

Oliver Goldsmith *The Deserted Village* (1770)

In 1662 the Act of Settlement had ruled that the parish was responsible only for those poor people born in it. Although much modified in later years, this act militated against the mobility of labour, and so it was often evaded in Norfolk. In 1723 an act recommended a parish workhouse and gave the Overseers powers to refuse relief unless a claimant entered it. Most parishes could not afford to build a workhouse, but in 1782 Gilbert's Act appointed Guardians of the Poor and encouraged parishes to form unions to build workhouses for the old, the sick and the orphans. In 1785 Worstead joined the Tunstead and Happing Incorporation, which built its House of Industry at Smallburgh. Little now survives of it except its farm buildings. The House provided for the old and sick of Worstead in a regime far more humane than that later prescribed in the New Poor Law of 1834. The able-bodied worked on the farm, ground flour on the treadmill (a job of work, not a punishment), dressed hemp, spun wool or worked in the house, which was well run and reasonably economical.

Fig 75. The site of Smallburgh Workhouse. (See www.workhouses.org.uk/Smallburgh)

During the French Wars of 1792-1815 the Poor Law Guardians chose to give outdoor relief to families who could not afford the rising price of bread, rather than pay for their keep in the Smallburgh House of Industry. In this they were supported by local farmers, who met 80% of the costs of outdoor relief but preferred to pay higher poor rates than higher wages which they might have to lower when prices fell. They also needed a pool of under-employed labour to call on at times of peak activity. Even though the Norfolk poor rates rose to £30,000 a year in 1832-34, the Guardians, most of them farmers, preferred to support low wages with outdoor relief until the 1860s and to encourage women and children to add to the family income by clearing stones, sowing wheat by dibbling, setting potatoes by hand, weeding crops with hoes, topping and tailing root crops, and so on.

King's Charity devoted a small fraction of its funds to the relief of poverty but the will of Charles Themilthorpe, signed in 1721, established a charity designed to give serious help to the poor. A board over the south door of St Mary's states *Charles Themilthorpe by will dated 1721 gave to such of the poor of Worstead as are not Collectioners* [recipients of poor relief under the Elizabethan Poor Law?] *2s. of bread each week to be delivered each Sunday by the Churchwardens and Overseers (paid for by lands in Worstead).* The Themilthorpes owned properties in Worstead from Henry VIII's reign, if not earlier, and five Themilthorpe tombs grace the chancel floor of St Mary's.

9. The turnpike changes the route to Norwich

The road system of the parish seems to have changed little since the late sixteenth century, and the Worstead enclosure of 1827 made few changes. The main route to Norwich was down Ducker's Road (leave Worstead on the road to Westwick and take the first left after the railway bridge). There were milestones on the road, tipped over in 1940 lest they help German invaders. The stone recording eleven miles to Norwich survives, but that recording twelve miles has not been found, though George Smith reported seeing it on his way to war in 1940. The turnpike from Norwich to North Walsham changed the route. Approved by act of Parliament in 1797, the turnpike ran through Westwick, where the Westwick Arch (sadly demolished in 1981) was the entry to the estate of John Berney Petre, who made the road skirt his land. The tolls at North Walsham and Crostwick were initially let for £80 and £90 but later for £121 and £260: the road evidently made a decent profit, though these figures suggest the southern stretch was more used than the northern.

10. The North Walsham and Dilham Canal

The River Ant was navigable as far as Dilham in the Middle Ages, but the Norwich Cathedral Priory, which shipped grain from its manors in Martham and Hemsby in its own boat, did not move grain by river from its manor in Worstead. Was the boat's draught too great for the shallow river? Transport by the boat was then some 58% cheaper than cartage. It was the cost of road transport that prompted the building of the North Walsham and Dilham Canal *(30, - NHER 13534)*: the Norwich-North Walsham turnpike charged 8d. per half ton of coal per mile, so that the price of a ton of coal doubled between Norwich and North Walsham.

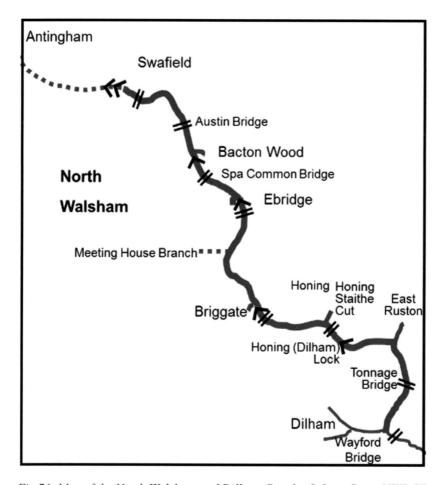

Fig 76 Map of the North Walsham and Dilham Canal – © Ivan Cane, NWDCT

In 1810 the proposal to make the Ant navigable from Dilham to Antingham Ponds was accepted by a public meeting. Plans for the canal were prepared, one by William Youard, two by John Millington. One of Millington's was chosen in 1811. People from Worstead and Dilham feared their businesses would suffer if boats could reach North Walsham, but despite their objections, a bill was submitted to Parliament and was enacted in 1812. The Act authorised the North Walsham and Dilham Canal Company to raise £30,000 by issuing shares and, if need be, a further £10,000 by shares or by mortgage. The canal's construction was delayed by more opposition, especially from Isaac Harris Lewis who feared that the trade of his staithe at Dilham would be damaged by the canal. The jury at the Quarter Sessions in April 1825 awarded him £1500 damages. Construction then began, directed by Thomas Hughes who had worked on several Scottish canals. It was not easy, for the course of the canal, which deviated in some places from the course of the River Ant, passed through some peaty and boggy ground. However, the first wherry reached Cubitt's Bacton Wood Mill on 14 June 1826 and the canal was formally opened on 29 August 1826 - at a total cost of £32,000.

Fig 77 Briggate Mill from the south-east 1926 © WWW.NorfolkMills.co.uk

The canal was worked mostly by wherries. The wherry was a flat bottomed boat with one square rigged sail and a hinged mast with a 1.5 ton counterweight to enable the sail to be lowered quickly to shoot the many bridges on Broadland rivers. Trading wherries had black sails and black hulls with a white prow for added visibility. Some wherries had a keel that could be quickly retracted or removed, which was necessary because the canal was little over a metre deep. If the wind was contrary, the sail was lowered and the wherry was quanted (punted) with a long pole or it was hauled by men, using what was called a 'hailing' path. There was no more substantial towpath, since the use of draught horses was never envisaged. The canal only took small wherries, no more than 3.7 metres wide, for its six locks were only 3.75 metres wide. The locks were at Honing, Briggate, Ebridge, Bacton Wood, and two at Swafield. They raised the canal by 18 metres over its full length of 8.2 miles from Tonnage Bridge in Dilham to Antingham Ponds. On the canal's banks were staithes for loading and unloading, and some important mills, the corn mills at Briggate, Ebridge, Bacton and Swafield, and the two bone mills at Antingham. There were two staithes in the parish of Worstead, one at Briggate, the other at Meeting Hill on a short spur from the main canal. The watermill at Briggate (*29 - NHER 8206*), the last in a probable series of mills on the site, had been built in the eighteenth century. It was driven by a breast-shot water wheel. Robert Colls, the miller in the late eighteenth century, would have used carts to transport his grain and flour, but John Balls, the miller in the 1830s, no doubt welcomed the opportunity to use the canal. Offal for the bone mills at Antingham was perhaps the most important cargo but coal, manure, feedcake, grain, flour and farm produce were also conveyed.

Fig 78 Briggate Mill in 2012 (now totally demolished)

11. The new Baptist Chapel at Meeting Hill

As farmers and their labourers struggled in the 1820s and 1830s, the Baptists of Meeting Hill embarked on an ambitious building programme, led by their pastor, Richard Clark (1813-32). The original meeting house in the barn had been improved, enlarged or even rebuilt in 1730 and had been doubled in size and been thatched in 1798 (NHER 16449); while a baptistry was built into it in 1824. Yet in the early decades of the nineteenth century the Baptists outgrew their old meeting house: in 1832 the membership stood at 152, but many more attended services.

Fig 79 Meeting Hill Baptist Church drawn by Mike McEwen © Worstead Parish Council

Six almshouses were built in 1820 thanks to the generosity of Samuel Chapman of Norwich, who may have been descended from Richard Culley through his daughter Sarah. The houses were designed for six to twelve poor persons. Each tenant was given £8 a year, financed by the rent from fifteen acres of land in Hellesdon. Preference was given to members of the church or of the congregation aged sixty or more, but once admitted a tenant might be ejected only for committing gross immorality, quarreling with neighbours or marrying someone under fifty. There were still some tricky issues. How might Mrs Flaxman have reacted to the bald note in a minute of 16 October

1891 *'Resolved that Mrs Flaxman be informed that Mrs Worship will go to live in the same cottage with her'*?

It was first proposed to replace the old meeting house in 1825, and the formal decision was taken in February 1829. In June the old chapel was demolished, an event commemorated by William Bullimore's poem *A farewell to the Old Meeting House at Worstead on its being taken down through decay*. Here are three of its sixteen verses:

> *For many years past Zion's mourners repaired*
> *And forgot their sorrow and pain,*
> *In finding the gospel a balm for their woes*
> *To cheer and revive them again.*
>
> *Here the Crucified Saviour, their Friend and their Lord,*
> *At his supper by faith has been seen;*
> *And hope, love and joy this temple have made*
> *A holy and heavenly scene.*
>
> *Their prayers unceasingly like incense arose*
> *And answers descended from heaven,*
> *Whilst converts appeared as the happy result*
> *And glory to Jesus was given.*

In June 1829 the foundations of the new square Chapel (*24* - NHER 17018) were dug and Zenas Trivett, then aged 76, laid the foundation stone and preached the sermon. Bricks from the old chapel were reused and more were made on site, and the Chapel was roofed with glazed black pantiles. The total cost was £882.10s, of which the minister Richard Clark gave £250 because - as a former successful businessman - he was, he said, *'blessed by an abundant harvest in life.'* On 6 October 1829 the first service was held in the new, light and airy building. In the same year stables for forty horses were built at a cost of £80, for many Baptists travelled some distance to worship in Meeting Hill.

12. Changes in St Mary's

The most noticeable additions to St Mary's are the many memorials in the floors and on the walls of St Mary's - too many to detail here, but ripe for recording and further research. For instance, at the east of the centre aisle we find William Bird, died 1814, aged 72, flanked by Elizabeth, his wife, died 1810, aged 71, and by Mary (born Bird?), wife of James Hardy, died 1775, aged 30. These and other Bird graves leave us with a family tree to disentangle; and there are many more. There are four hatchments, used in funerals from the seventeenth century. Over the south door is that of Robert Berney of Holly Grove House who died in 1828. Three hatchments of the Brograve family were once in the chancel but are now above the north door of the nave. There are two vaults below the floor. The entry to the Berney vault is before the door of the Lady Chapel and there are memorials to members of the very priestly family in the floor before the rood screen and on the chancel and south aisle walls. In the chancel floor is the entry to the Brograve vault, constructed in 1766 by Berney Brograve. There is an opening low down in the east end exterior wall of the chancel through which lead coffins can be seen.

Fig 80 One of the Brograve hatchments now above the north door of the nave.

In 1831 the screen below the western gallery and ringing chamber was repainted by Mrs S E Gunn, wife of the Vicar of Irstead and good friend of the wife of Worstead's Vicar. She copied the representation of the seven virtues created by Sir Joshua Reynolds for the chapel windows of New College, Oxford: Faith, Charity, Fortitude, Patience, Learning, Hope, Justice, and Prudence. Her colour scheme differs from his and she may have worked from a black and white picture of Sir Joshua's windows. Above the screen is the ringing chamber, which has remarkably wide floor timbers. The planks are contemporary with the screen which dates from 1501 and they are inscribed with some interesting graffiti which deserve to be further explored. Only the largest bell survived the confiscation of 1552. Change-ringing, introduced in the late sixteenth century, led to many churches having eight bells by the eighteenth. By then St Mary's had the six bells it has now, all cast in the Norwich Bell-Foundry: the third in 1640, the fifth in 1645, the treble in 1675, the sixth in 1706, the second in 1722 and the fourth in 1723. The bells rang out on many special occasions, notably for the victory at Culloden in 1746 and the state funeral of Admiral Lord Nelson in 1806.

Fig 81 'I Tell All That A Man at Brakindel Did New Make Me.1722'

13. Curates for St Mary's from the Paston School

Charles Forder, a pupil at the Paston School in 1919-25, was the youngest son of Henry and Mary-Ann Forder, who lived in Forge Cottage, where Henry plied his trade as a blacksmith. Like two of his eighteenth century predecessors - John, son of John Ashmul, grazier of Worstead, at Paston in 1767-69; and John, son of William Bird, grocer of Worstead, at Paston in 1778-85 - he went up to Cambridge and was ordained. He then served in parishes in the north of England and became Archdeacon of York. His *History of the Paston School*, published in 1934 and revised in 1975, details the Masters (later Headmasters). Many of them were ordained and some became curates in Worstead:

Joseph Hepworth (Master in 1778-95) in 1788-1800
Joseph's nephew, William Hepworth (Usher or Assistant Master)
      around 1791
Henry Hunter (Master in 1796-1807) in 1800-03
William Tylney Spurdens (Master 1807-25) in 1837-40
Thomas Dry (Master in 1844-73) in 1856-68.

14. Schooling in late Georgian Worstead

Five private day schools, sometimes called dame schools if run by a woman, were reported to exist in Worstead in 1833. They were probably quite small. Teachers are mentioned but none is linked to a specific school:

Edmund Starling in 1819
Richard Tuck in 1826 and 1828
Charles Sumner in 1830
John Barnard in Briggate in 1819, 1836 and 1841
William Woodrow in Meeting House Hill in 1836.

More significant in size were the Anglican and Baptist Sunday schools. The Baptist Sunday School dated from 1815 and in the 1820s benefited from the teaching of John Rix Blakely, who later became the minister (1832/33-1837). No start date has been found for the Anglican Sunday School. Both were flourishing in 1851, when the Religious Census returns reported sixty-three Baptist scholars and seventy-one Anglican. The primary role of Sunday schools was to teach Christian belief and morality. Many also taught reading to give pupils access to the *Bible* and some taught writing and arithmetic.

Fig 82 Front Street c 1900 Courtesy Mr B Hedge, Worstead

5. VICTORIAN AND EDWARDIAN WORSTEAD

1. Worstead in the Religious Census of 1851

The Religious Census offers us a snapshot of religious worship in Worstead on 30 March 1851. The Census aimed to quieten the fears of many Victorians that machines and factories were creating godless cities and to reassure religious groups who felt threatened. Nonconformists thought that Anglicans were denying them equal civil and religious rights. Anglicans feared that the Nonconformists would soon outnumber them. Evangelicals saw Anglican converts to Rome as proof that the Tractarians, who favoured a more Catholic (but not Roman Catholic) worship in the Church of England, were a Roman fifth column in the Established Church. And most Protestants were enraged when in 1850 the Pope re-established a hierarchy of Roman Catholic bishops in England and Wales. The Census asked each place of religious worship: to what denomination do you belong; when was your place of worship built; how many seats does it have; how many are free, how many rented; and how many attendances were there on Census Sunday, 30 March 1851?

Worstead's 'ancient parish church' was recorded as endowed with a commuted tithe of £270 with 'other permanent endowment' of £10, fees of £2.10s, and other income of £2. The tithe commutation had been agreed in 1843 and the tithe map in 1844: a commuted tithe of £618 went to the impropriators (essentially the Dean and Chapter of the Cathedral) and £270.9s.6d to the vicar. In 1851 St Mary's had 500 sittings, 300 of them free: pew rents were evidently still levied, if only on 200 seats. On 30 March the attenders totalled 87 adults and 71 Sunday scholars in the morning; 245 adults and 71 Sunday scholars in the afternoon; and 106 adults in the evening: a total of 580 attendances. The Vicar, the Rev George King, claimed that the average attendances Sunday by Sunday were 120 and 80 in the morning, 240 and 80 in the afternoon, and 250 in the evening: a total of 770, some 190 higher than the actual attendances on Census Sunday. George King explained the difference by remarking '*Sickness is very prevalent at this time.*' Was he deceiving himself?

Unfortunately the Census counted attendances, not people: a person who attended two or three times counted as two or three attendances. Imagine a village with one Anglican church and a population of 100. The vicar counts 60 attendances, an attendance of 60% according to Horace Mann who analysed the figures. But there were two services: 20 people went twice (40 attendances) and 20 went once (20 attendances), making a total of 60 attendances. Yet only 40 villagers went to church, and so only 40% of the population worshipped on that Sunday. To turn attendances into worshippers Mann counted morning attendances as if they were all worshippers and added half of the afternoon's and a third of the evening's. So Mann's figures for St Mary's would be 158 in the morning, 158 in the afternoon and 35 in the evening, that is 351 worshippers. Nonconformists objected, because their main service was usually in the afternoon or evening. So today's historians usually add the attendances of the best attended service (316 in the afternoon) to one third of the attendances at any other services (53 in the morning, 35 in the evening), giving a total of 404 worshippers in St Mary's, roughly half Worstead's population of 827 - a goodly number and a little better than the national average. These Anglican figures cannot be compared with those of the Baptist Chapel in Meeting Hill, because most of the Baptists lived outside the parish.

John Webb, the Baptist minister in 1849-58, reported the attendances on 30 March: 177 adults and 63 Sunday scholars in the morning, 319 and 63 in the afternoon, and 100 adults in the evening. These 722 attendances probably represented 495 people (411 adults and 84 Sunday scholars) spread across three services. John Webb said the average attendances '*in the summer months*' were 230 and 90 in the morning and 400 and 90 in the afternoon. The 300 free sittings and 230 other sittings, presumably subject to pew rents, were evidently needed.

2. Innovation and restoration in St Mary's

At the time of the Census the chancel of St Mary's was being reordered. The new arrangement owed much to the renewed interest in ritual which was prompted by the Oxford Movement, launched in 1833. Its first followers were called Tractarians, who sought a return to more ceremonial worship in churches that were restored to what they saw as their medieval Gothic splendour. So St Mary's altar and sanctuary were raised to draw all eyes to the centrality of the eucharist. The carved stone altar was erected in 1843 by the Vicar, John Thurlow.

The stone altar rails and reredos were added in 1848 and 1850, probably requiring the sill of the east window to be raised. These changes were funded by the Wharton Trust, which also paid for the carved oak stalls. The pulpit and reading desk were added in 1852-53. A new organ was installed in 1851 at a cost of £120 raised by public subscription, but was replaced in 1879 by a better organ which cost £250.

Fig 83 The re-ordering of the Chancel

There was some restoration of the Lady Chapel in 1878 and of the chancel in 1891, but major work on the roof in 1899-1900 cost £1100. The wall posts of the nave roof end in corbels which bear heraldic shields. Most of the shields relate to the nineteenth century.

On **the south side from east to west** are the arms of:

Norwich Cathedral: Norwich Cathedral gained the rectory of St Mary's in the Middle Ages and in the nineteenth century the patronage was exercised by the Dean and Chapter for two turns and the Bishop for one turn.

Fig 84

Rous: the Rous family owned the Worstead Estate from 1828 to 1938.

Fig 85

Prior Lovely [or Loveday?]: as yet unidentified.

Fig 86

Themylthorpe: Charles Themylthorpe founded the charity which still bore his name in 1899-1900.

Fig 87

Marsham: as yet unidentified.

Fig 88

Brograve: Sir Thomas Brograve married Julian Berney and their son inherited most of her father John's Worstead lands.

Fig 89

Berney: John Berney was the father of Julian (see above).

Fig 90

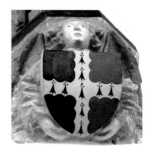

Sedgwick: Adam Sedgwick was Professor of Geology at Cambridge and Residentiary Canon of Norwich 1833-73.

Fig 91

Norwich Cathedral impaling Goulburn: Edward Goulburn was Dean of Norwich in 1866-88.

Fig 92

More of the heraldic shields on the **north side** refer back to St Mary's earlier history, but others have nineteenth century connections. From **west to east** are the arms of :

The See of Norwich impaling Pelham: John Thomas Pelham was Bishop of Norwich in 1857-93.

Fig 93

Thurlow: John Thurlow was the Vicar of Worstead in 1841-44

Fig 94

Wharton: The Rev Henry Wharton founded the charity that bears his name.

Fig 95

Arblaster: John Alblaster or Arblaster, named on the rood screen, came from the family recorded in Worstead in the *Domesday Book*.

Fig 96

Stapleton: The Stapleton family owned land in medieval Worstead and Ingham. Sir Miles Stapleton (1319-64), a Knight of the Garter, founded the Trinitarian Priory of Ingham and is buried there.
Fig 97

Bishop Walter de Suffield: Suffield was Bishop of Norwich in 1244-57.
Fig 98

The See of Norwich: The Bishop of Norwich shared the patronage of St Mary's with the Dean and Chapter.
Fig 99

St Benet's Abbey: The *Little Domesday Book* records the Priory of St Benet's at Holme as the owner of most of Worstead and of both its churches in 1066.
Fig 100

Petre: The Petre family inherited the Westwick
Estate from John Berney via his daughter Elizabeth.

Fig 101

3 The completion of the Baptist settlement

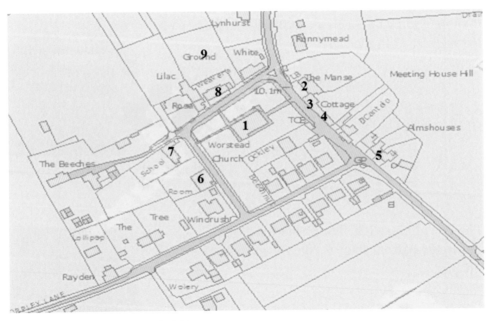

Fig 102 Map of Meeting Hill 2015
1 The Chapel from 1829, 2 The Manse, 3 The Caretaker's Cottage, 4 The Stables, 5 The Almshouses, 6 The School, 7 Schoolmaster's House, 8 The Weaver's Cottage, 9 The original chapel site and burial ground.

The numbers in the Religious Census justified the new building that had just taken place in Meeting Hill. Galleries were added to the chapel in 1843. In 1844 the chapel was extended to included a ground floor vestry and a first floor Schoolroom to accommodate the Sunday School and the new day school of the British and Foreign Schools Society (see section 4 below). The *Manual of the Baptist Church in Worstead* of 1898 records that Richard Clark gave £100 for the vestry and the schoolroom: his gift was taken from the benefactions that featured in his will. In 1844 the current frontage of the

Manse was added to a seventeenth/eighteenth century house. At the same time the Caretaker's Cottage (now the Manse Cottage) was built to offer facilities for Baptists who spent the whole of Sunday at the Chapel. A room on its upper floor, accessible from the upstairs of the Manse, served as the minister's office. In 1848 the Schoolmaster's House was built and in 1854 the New Schoolroom, since the Old Schoolroom, only built 1844, was too small for the sixty boys and forty girls of the British School. The buildings remain largely unaltered, but a new Miller organ from America was installed in the Chapel in 1882, causing the adoption of the Baptist hymnbook *Psalms and Hymns* a year later (a copy recently found in a charity shop is inscribed: *Baptist Sunday School, Worstead. Presented to Nellie Amies for regular attendance 1922. Feb 28th '23.* Did Nellie live in the parish? An Amies family lived at Rookery Farm, now Swan's Farm, in the 1920s). In 1886 the Chapel was re-seated to accommodate 500 worshippers at a cost of £300, though numbers were beginning to fall by then. The outstanding cluster of buildings created by the Baptists of Meeting Hill in the nineteenth century deserves far greater recognition.

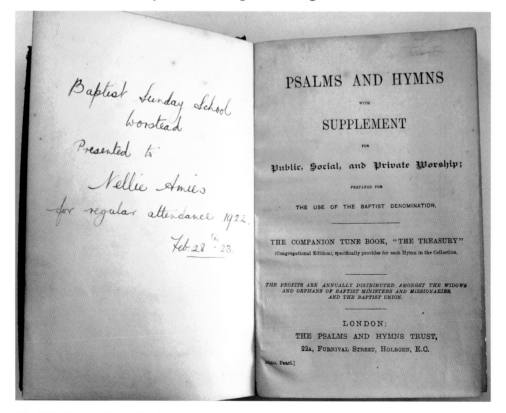

Fig 103 Baptist Hymn Book

4. The outreach of Worstead Baptist Church

Under Richard Clark Worstead Baptist Church had helped to found new churches at Ludham in 1821 and Bacton in 1822. It had been involved in the Norfolk and Suffolk Baptist Association since 1769/70, but was happy to become part of the East Norfolk Baptist Association, founded in 1828 at a meeting in Aylsham and extended to the whole county in 1834, when Worstead probably joined. The Norfolk Association affiliated to the national Baptist Union in 1836, but became divided over a number of issues, chiefly over whether the celebration of the Lord's Supper should be open to Christians who lacked an adult believer's baptism. Since their separation from the General Baptists, Norfolk's Particular Baptists had practised closed communion, but most now chose open communion, St Mary's in Norwich in 1857 and Worstead in 1858, when a church meeting resolved:

...That this Church, while steadfastly maintaining that believers' baptism by immersion is a scriptural ordinance, yet not regarding it as necessary to salvation, does hereby welcome to the Lord's Table all whom it believes to be joint partakers with it in the Grace of Christ, whether immersed or not.

...That this Church reserves to itself the right to use the the same means to satisfy itself of the piety of candidates for communion as of those for baptism and Church fellowship.

...That members of other Christian Churches holding the fundamental doctrines of the Bible, be admitted to occasional communion in the same way as members of other Baptist Churches.

A court action to impose closed communion on all Particular Baptists failed in 1860, and those who maintained closed communion formed a separate denomination of Strict and Particular Baptists. Few Norfolk churches joined it: the nearest was at Salhouse. In 1862 the Norfolk Association of Particular Baptists was reconstituted. It met in Meeting Hill in 1883, and its agenda gives an insight into the concerns of late Victorian Particular Baptists: evangelistic services; the position and prospects of village churches; the importance of relationships with other Christian communities; and the principles, privileges and obligations of Voluntaries (the churches and religious societies which had to fund themselves).

Richard Barcham Shalders was born in 1824 at Norwich House to the Baptists Phoebe (née Barcham) and Jacob Shalders. In 1847 Richard joined the committee of the London Young Men's Christian Association, itself formed in 1844. In 1851 he married Eliza Rooke at the Chapel in Meeting Hill and the newly-weds emigrated aboard the *Katherine Stewart Forbes* to Auckland, New Zealand. Arriving in March 1852, Richard followed in the footsteps of his father Jacob in Worstead and set up a drapery business in Auckland. He began to hold scripture classes in April 1853, and was the driving force behind the foundation of the first New Zealand branch of the YMCA in 1855. Its first building in Auckland was opened in 1856. A remarkable Christian person, an excellent speaker and an inspiring teacher, he dedicated over 60 years of his life to instructing young working men. In 1912 he wrote a booklet *The Early History of the Auckland Young Men's Christian Association*. He died aged 90 in 1914.

5. Worstead Baptist Church in 1898

After John Webb came a succession of Baptist ministers who served the church well: J F Smythe 1858-66, W H Payne 1867-73, Walter W Laskey 1874-80, John Jackson 1880-96 and Arthur Spelman Culley 1896-1912. Arthur Culley was a descendant of the founding pastor in Meeting Hill, Richard Culley. In 1898 he revised and updated the *Manual of the Baptist Church in Worstead* originally written by the Rev J F Smythe in 1859, when the church had 140 members. A hundred bound copies and fifty unbound were printed for sale at cost price to members. In 1898 there were seventy-nine members, something of a decline. Most of them lived outside the parish of Worstead. Only eleven members lived in Meeting Hill:

Elizabeth Debbage	John Delf
Susanna Delf	Maria Flaxman
Sarah Flaxman	Sarah Roper
Elizabeth Rump	Jane Turner
Charlotte Woodhouse	Mary Wodehouse
Mary Ann Wright	

Another Meeting Hill member, Elizabeth Webster, had died in 1896. Two members lived in Briggate: Ann Watts and Elizabeth Webster. Samuel Mason was a member from Worstead Town, but three members from there had died recently: Mary Worship in 1897, Sarah Andrews and Phoebe Hewitt in 1898. Other members lived in North Walsham (27), White Horse Common (7), Honing (6) Westwick (4), Burgh next Aylsham (3), Neatishead (2), Paston (2), Antingham (1), Dilham (1), East Ruston (1) Ingworth (1), Skeyton (1), Stalham (1), and Tunstead (1). A further six were described as non-resident.

In 1898 the Pastor, Arthur Culley, was President of the Sunday School and of the Band of Hope. The Deacons were Edwin Learner (also Church Treasurer), James Wright, Edward Burton, Thomas Allen (also a Seat Steward), Ernest Burton (also a Seat Steward), and John Youngman (also Vice-President of the Band of Hope). The Superintendents of the Sunday School were Edwin Learner and George Smart, and its Treasurer was Mrs Edwin (Catherine) Learner. The Band of Hope, a branch of a national temperance organisation aiming to teach children about the evils of alcoholic drink, was run by a committee: Arthur Culley (President), John Youngman (Vice-President), Mrs Edwin Learner, Miss Edith Stedman (Secretary), Mrs Mary Ann Cross, Mrs (Rebecca or Lilian?) Davison, and Miss (Rosa?) Watson.

Sunday by Sunday Divine Service began at 10.30 am and 2.30 pm, with a Gospel Service at 7.00 pm in the summer. The Lord's Supper was administered at the end of the afternoon service on the first Sunday of the month. An evening service was held every Wednesday at 7.00 or 7.30 pm according to the season. The Sunday School met at 9.30 am and 1.30 pm, and the Band of Hope at 7.00 pm on Mondays. The Chapel was licensed for weddings and the graveyard was for the use of church members and the congregation. Church Meetings were held as required after giving a week's notice. It was in 1898 that weekly offerings were introduced.

Seven pages of the Manual are devoted to the personal, family, church and world duties of a Christian, defined in a way that any late Victorian Evangelical would accept: each of the eighty-three duties is supported by reference to biblical texts, more from the *Epistles* than from the *Gospels*.

6. Worstead's Primitive Methodist Chapel

The records of the Baptists of Meeting Hill hint at competition from the Methodists in the later eighteenth century and from the growing number of Methodist denominations in the nineteenth. The Primitive Methodists outgrew the Wesleyans and all the other Methodist denominations in nineteenth century Norfolk. They attracted farm labourers and manual workers for four main reasons. First, they rejected tithes. Few members paid them, because tithes were largely paid by landowners, but one of the farm workers' complaints from about 1830 was that high tithes levied on farmers kept the wages of their employees low. Second, the Primitives were often willing to host agricultural trade union meetings in their chapels: George Edwards, a leading light in Norfolk trade unionism and a Labour MP in the 1920s, was a Primitive Methodist. Third, they offered lively, revivalist worship and activities at the chapel every night of the week, such as prayer meetings, women's and men's meetings, class meetings, and missionary lectures. Fourth, they provided practical support in clothing, coal and savings clubs and created funds to help needy members. In these ways they gave meaning and support to the hard life of farm labourers. As a result the Primitive Methodists were still expanding and building some new chapels when most other Victorian denominations had stopped building once their relative decline became evident in the later 1880s. However the support that the Primitives gave to farm workers attracted the hostility of the mostly Anglican farmers and landowners.

Fig 104 Primitive Baptist Chapel, Honing Row.(Foundation stone inset.)

The account book of Worstead's Primitive Methodist Chapel in the Norfolk Record Office dates from the later nineteenth century and includes *A Reminiscence of Years Gone By.* This appears to have been written by James Benjamin Copping, the grocer, draper and postmaster of Norwich House Stores from the late nineteenth century into the twentieth. The earliest Primitive Methodist Society in Worstead was apparently formed around 1846. It escaped the notice of the local enumerator who identified churches and chapels for the Census of Religious Worship in 1851: some other congregations in Norfolk were likewise omitted from the Census. The Society worshipped in a rented cottage, perhaps the unidentified building later called the Old Ranters' Chapel, and it also ran a temperance society. Supported by the local circuit, the Worstead Society sought a site to build a chapel but was frustrated by the superior buying power of one leading landowner (unnamed), while approaches to other landowners were equally unavailing. Eventually the Primitive Methodists found '*There was one little spot in the centre of the enemy's country that the petty Land Tyrant could not withhold from the Lord's people, the same spot where sweet stuff had been dispensed from the Village shop for two Centuries. [A part of it] was ... now to be consecrated to the Lord of hosts for the sole use of his own people. A Trust was formed and means were taken (with the most gratifying results) for collecting the needful funds.*' The foundation stone was laid on 6 July 1892 by Robert Price of London during the ministry of the Rev J Buck. On that day James Benjamin Copping, a trustee of the chapel, made a gift of 10s, not far off a week's wages for an farm labourer, and wrote '*The Lord told me to give up part of my premises next the highway* [Honing Row] *whereon to build a House to His Holy name.*' The Chapel (*4*) cost £290 and was opened in the same year.

7. Worstead's Victorian schools

In 1851 the Religious Census counted 39,882 scholars in 696 Sunday schools in Norfolk, but failed to include all the 774 Sunday schools that then existed. These figures compare with 34,961 Norfolk pupils in 497 public day schools and 18,745 pupils in 864 private day schools. Some of the public day schools were charity schools, provided by societies such as the Society for the Propagation of Christian Knowledge (SPCK) founded in 1698 or by local initiatives. However by the mid nineteenth century most were run by the voluntary religious societies. The largest was the Anglican National Society, founded in 1811, which had 360 of the 497 public day schools in Norfolk in 1851. The next largest voluntary society, the Nonconformist British Society founded in 1808, had only forty-nine. By 1851 both Societies were sponsoring schools in the parish of Worstead.

Mr C.T. Keen succeeded William Humphrey (1839-43) as the Baptist pastor in 1843 (at a good annual salary of £100). He wished to start a day school of the Nonconformist British and Foreign Schools Society and a year later the British School in Meeting Hill opened, charging each pupil 2d. a week. No doubt the school taught the 4 Rs: religion, reading, writing and arithmetic, as well as more practical skills, needlework for the girls and perhaps cookery, and probably gardening for the boys. In 1845 George Matthews was the Master, presumably the first; Mary Ann Julen was the Mistress in 1850; and Joseph and Mary Ann Helsdon were the Master and Mistress by 1854 and served for seventeen years. The school was still open in 1883, but not in 1898, when the *Manual* of the Baptist Church merely says the school '*was carried on for some years.*' It probably did not long survive the new climate created by the Education Act of 1870, which the Baptists opposed.

Fig 105 Worstead National School

Planning for a National School in Worstead began in the 1830s, when Worstead's major landowners, the Honourable William Rufus Rous of Worstead, Mr Jack Petre of Westwick, and the Honourable William Postle of Smallburgh agreed to raise money for it. The cost was estimated at £309 with a further £23.14s.3d. allowed for furniture and equipment. The building was designed to accommodate seventy-five boys and seventy-five girls in two classrooms, giving each pupil six square feet of space. It was a basic building, with only two coal fires for heating, oil lamps for lighting, and outdoor privies. £150 was soon promised and a grant of £80 was expected from the Education Department. The plot of land, only 25 x 17 metres, was the gift of the Rous family, who in 1845 conveyed it to the Vicar George

King and the Dean George Pellew of Norwich and their successors. The school, designed by R M Phipson, the County and Diocesan Surveyor, was erected and opened in 1845, a year later than the British School in Meeting Hill. The opening of Worstead School (*20*) caused the fair to move to Church Plain and Ruin Road, until rowdy behaviour led to its demise in 1912.

The schoolmaster's house was built in front of Worstead School in 1854 in a style reminiscent of the Elizabethan or Jacobean period, used for the new vicarage (now Peverel House) erected in 1844-45 and extended in 1848. The cost, just over £354, exceeded the estimate of £300.

George Evans was described in the baptismal register as a schoolmaster, when he and his wife Harriet had their three children baptised in St Mary's on 23 November 1845: were William Patrick George, Mary Elizabeth and Harriet Keturah of differing ages or might they have been triplets? Triplets were known in Worstead: those born to Robert and Elizabeth Day died within a week of their birth and were buried on 28 August 1796. If - as seems likely - George Evans were the Master of the National School, he could hardly leave his children unbaptised. By 1850 John Cosby was listed as the Master and in 1854 John Wilding, and in 1871 the census described Reuben and Edith Moss as the National School Master and Mistress.

Parents paid 1d. a week, more than the poorest families could afford. From the 1840s to the 1860s Her Majesty's Inspectors often complained of absences caused by children working in field gangs and of the closure of the school from early August to early November for the harvest. In rural parishes like Worstead seasonal demand for agricultural labour affected school attendance until the late nineteenth century despite the legislation outlined below. The only Worstead children assured of absolutely regular schooling were inmates of the Smallburgh House of Industry who were taught in a special classroom in Smallburgh School.

The British and National Schools would have been competition for Worstead's private day schools. These included the dame school conducted in the Georgian farmhouse Benefield House (*12)* perhaps by Maria Rump, who appears in the 1841 census as a schoolmistress in Shalders' Yard, the former name of Swann's Yard. Harriet Taylor of Briggate was described as a teacher in the same census. Aged fifteen she could not have been a pupil teacher, because the scheme was not introduced until 1846. We may think her too young to be a teacher, but other young people were all earning their living at her age. In 1845 *Kelly's Directory* indicates that she taught at what was called the Ladies' School in association with C Taylor (perhaps her older sister). In 1854 the Ladies' School was run by Taylor and Newbiggin. Did one of the Taylors marry? Mrs Elizabeth Taylor's name follows the school entry in 1845 and 1854. Was she the mother of Harriet and her sister, and was the school based in her house? In 1850 and 1854 another Ladies' School (day and boarding) was run by the Misses Smith in Holly Grove House. Other people are recorded as teachers but their schools are not specified: James Holt and Sarah Ann Kirk in 1861, Mercy Cross and Mary A Gibbs in 1871, and William Elliott Amies in 1872.

Fig 106 Benefield House drawn by Mike NcEwen © Worstead Parish Council

Forster's Education Act of 1870 aimed to create a national education system that was acceptable to the voluntary religious societies but also accommodated those who wanted secular schooling. So it tried to fill the gaps left by the voluntary societies by requiring that where no efficient school existed a school board should be formed to provide one. The education in board schools was to be non-denominational. The 1870 Act did not apply to Worstead because it already had two efficient schools, but other government legislation soon began to affect all schools. An act in 1873 forbade field work under the age of eight. In 1876 Sandon's Act forbade employment under the age of ten, set up school attendance committees in areas which had no school board, and gave the committees and boards the power to compel attendance. In 1880 Mundella's Act made attendance compulsory for those aged five to ten and for those aged ten to thirteen if attendance and achievement had been unsatisfactory. By 1891 elementary schooling was all but free. The leaving age was raised to eleven in 1893, to twelve in 1899, and to fourteen in 1918. In the early 1890s a new classroom was added to Worstead school for up to sixty infants at a cost of £354. By 1902 the attendance at the school averaged 117. In 1883 Miss Rudd is recorded as its Mistress. In 1896 the staff consisted of C Dyball and E Brown, both certificated teachers; M Brockway, assistant teacher; and B Scott, pupil teacher. *Kelly's Directory* names Miss Dyball as the Mistress in 1902 and Arthur Townsend as the Master in 1904. By 1912 Arthur W Calthorpe was described as the school's Headmaster.

By then Balfour's Act of 1902 had abolished school boards, created Local Education Authorities (the Counties and County Boroughs) and gave them authority over all elementary schools (the old board and voluntary schools) and the duty to provide secondary schools. The secondary grammar schools for Worstead were the Paston School and North Walsham High School for Girls. Worstead School became an elementary school of the sort described as *non-provided*, which meant that the school was run on the rates but the Church of England's governors still owned the building and had charge of religious education.

8. High farming from the 1840s to the mid 1870s

No doubt the *'petty Land Tyrant'* enjoyed the good times that returned for farmers in the 1840s. 'High farming' relied on high investment and was reckoned to be suited to farms above 300 acres, but in the census of 1851 only sixty-three Norfolk farmers held 300 acres or more. Even so, the good loams of Sloley, Worstead's near neighbour, were said in 1837 to be high farmed. Did high farming reach Worstead? Quite possibly, although Worstead farmers, like so many across Norfolk, may have stuck to their four course rotation, while improving on the older methods of the Agrarian Revolution.

Land was drained with porous pottery pipes, mass-produced from the 1840s, though most sherds of field drains found on Worstead's fields are more modern. From the 1830s guano (sea-bird dung from South America) and bone meal (from the bone mills at Antingham via the North Walsham and Dilham Canal) were used to fertilise the fields. In the 1840s and 1850s chemical fertilisers (nitrates, potash and super-phosphates) became available but were little used in Norfolk until the twentieth century. New machinery was bought. The horse-drawn reaper, invented in the 1820s-30s, replaced the scythe after the Great Exhibition of 1851. In turn it gave way to the reaper-binder in the 1880s. From the 1850s steam power, already used in industry and on railways, was applied to ploughing and threshing. In Worstead the 1861 census described George Watts as a farm (traction) engine driver and in 1904 Sidney Cross was the proprietor of mobile threshing machines, which were driven by belts from traction engines.

Selective breeding led to two new breeds. In the 1860s the black-faced Norfolk Horn sheep was crossed with the Southdown to produce the Suffolk. The Suffolk Polled cow, noted for the quality of its butter, was crossed with the Norfolk blood-red bull, famed for its quicker fattening. The resulting Norfolk and Suffolk Red Polled cattle was recognised as a breed in 1863 and became known as Red Poll cattle. By 1850 Smithfield sold three times as many cattle as it did in 1750, many fattened in Norfolk. They were driven in a week to London, losing 28 lb in weight, until after 1845 trains from Norwich to London cut out the walk. Did Worstead Fair play its part in this trade in livestock? In 1845 Meeting Hill had a cattle dealer in John Goose.

Fig 107 Gothic Lodge Sloley Road

That the farmers made profits is suggested by further changes to Manor Farm barns and to other farm buildings across the parish. The fine estate cottage of Gothic Lodge on Sloley Road (*35* - NHER 47380) belongs to this period. The mid nineteenth century also saw the construction of Worstead Mill (*25* - NHER 11731), the tall brick tower mill that stands between Briggate and Meeting Hill. By 1904 it was operated by Cubitt & Walker. Last used in 1922, it kept its sails into the 1930s and still retains its boat-shaped cap, its fantail cradle and brake wheel shaft. It was the last of a long line of windmills across the parish from perhaps as early as the thirteenth century. The field name *Mill Hill* suggests that there was once a windmill on the high point near the junction of Station Road and Westwick Road. On the map of 1781 copied from one of c.1600 a post-mill (*36* - NHER 18019) is marked in what is now the south-west corner of Worstead Park. On Faden's Map of Norfolk of 1797 a windmill, probably Worstead Old Mill, stood near Briggate Mill: this post-mill was demolished in 1812. At Briggate watermill (*29* - NHER 8206) the millers in 1845 (Christopher Sadler) and in 1854 (Jonathan Roe) used water power alone, but by 1902 the millers, Cubitt & Walker, who bought the mill in 1871, were using both water and steam power.

Fig 108 Worstead Mill 2012

In the period of high farming the pay of farm labourers rose to 10s. or 11s. a week (with a harvest wage of £5 to £7), but they still had less to spend on food than labourers in many counties. In an over-stocked labour market farmers were reluctant to raise wages that they might have to cut if the price of corn fell. Many farm workers still lived in hovels, described in William Cobbett's *Rural Rides* of 1830 as *'made of mud, straw, bits of glass and cast-off windows.'* Only the more fortunate lived in the small brick and flint cottages built in the mid nineteenth century.

9. Farming in the Great Depression from c.1875 to 1914

Poor harvests in 1873-9 and serious outbreaks of disease in both cattle and sheep heralded the start of a long depression in farming. By 1873 England already imported 50% of its cereals and 14% of its meat, but increased competition from abroad undermined production at home: cheaper cereals, meat and wool were produced on a large scale in America, Canada, Argentina, New Zealand and Australia, and carried cheaply to Britain by steamships, some of them refrigerated. Prices fell: wheat averaged 16s. a hundredweight in 1855, 10s.6d in 1875, 7s.8d. in 1885 and 5s.5d in 1895. Prices recovered a little in the early 1900s but only rose substantially during World War I, when foreign supplies were interrupted. In 1870-1914 the national acreage of arable land fell from 15,000,000 to 11,000,000, while the acreage of pasture land rose from 11,000,000 to 16,000,000, as farmers turned to producing fresh meat and milk. James Burton, a farmer in 1904, is listed as a dairyman in Withergate in 1912. Other farmers turned to fruit and vegetables: Cross & Suffling, grocers in 1904, were market gardeners at Lyngate Lodge in 1912. Some farmers, especially those on heavy land, went bankrupt. The aristocracy declined as rents overall fell by 50% in 1874-96 and rents on good land by 25%. Though times were hard for farmers, their numbers in Worstead remained reasonably steady: twelve are listed in *White's Directory of Norfolk* in 1854; eleven in *Kelly's Directory of Norfolk* in 1904, but only eight and a dairyman in 1912.

Farmers in the parish in 1854	Farmers in 1904
Thomas Boult (Worstead)	Robert Amies
Robert Colk (Worstead)	ET Learner
Henry Cook (Withergate)	Albert John Burton
Thomas Cross (Brockley)	James Burton
Joseph Durrell (Sand Hill)	George Coldham
Robert Greenacre (Bengate)	Frederick William Cross
John Lacey (Worstead)	Thomas Robert Cross
Henry Loveday (Withergate)	Henry Grix

William Nash (Bengate)   Walter F Newton (Manor Farm)
Henry Watts (Worstead)   Edwin Thomas Self
Mary Weldon (Brockley)   Matthew Weldon (Bunns Farm)
William Woodrow (Brockley)

Each of these farmers is worthy of further investigation. For instance in the census of 1841 Robert Greenacre, aged 35, was a farmer in Bengate with his wife Charlotte, also aged 35. Robert and Charlotte then had seven children (Robert 15, Charles 14, Ann 11, Louisa 8, George 6, Simon 3, and Anna 1); and they also had a servant, Mary Loads aged 15. In 1861 the family was still living in Bengate and farming 170 acres, by Norfolk standards a substantial holding. Of the children only Simon, aged 23, Anna, aged 20, and Jane, aged 18, were still living in the farmhouse: Jane had not been born in 1841. The family evidently left Bengate before 1871.

The major landholdings still belonged to the same families. In 1875 Lieutenant Colonel William John Rous inherited the Worstead Estate. Educated at Eton, he was wounded three times during the Crimean War of 1853-56. He never married, but was a well-known horticulturalist, a lover of country sports, a great traveller, and a strong Conservative. The report of his funeral in the *Eastern Daily Press* on 18 April 1914 suggests he was well-connected in society but was also a kind employer and a generous benefactor. In 1904 he was managing the Estate with his farm bailiff (William Disdale), his head gardener (William Chittleborough) and his head gamekeeper (Absolom Pattle). The other major landowners in 1902 were Mrs Petre of Westwick House, the trustees of the late John Seaman Postle of Smallburgh (replaced by Mrs Lubbock - presumably born Postle - in 1904), and Henry Morse Taylor JP of the Rookery in Dilham.

Norfolk's farm labourers found life hard. Despite the Depression wages did improve somewhat to 11s, 12s or even 13s. a week, with a harvest wage of £6 to £7. This rise was helped by the farm workers' trade unions that emerged after 1872; by an act in 1873 which forbade the employment of children under eight on the land; by acts in 1876 and 1880 which made school compulsory at least to the age of ten; and perhaps most crucially by at least one farm worker in ten leaving the land between 1871 and 1891. Worstead's population had grown from 650 to 830 in 1801-31 (if more slowly than that of Norfolk and of England), had leveled off at 827 by 1851, but then fell to 819 in 1891, 781 in 1901, and 747 in 1911. Some left for work in northern industrial towns: two thirds of Norfolk people chose the worsted-making West Riding of Yorkshire. Others emigrated under a scheme created by the New Poor Law of 1834: 3,354 left Norfolk in 1835-7, most for Canada but some for Australia. Towards the end of the nineteenth century and up to World War I emigration to the Empire and the USA became popular, especially among young men (42% of emigrants in 1871-1911 were males aged 18-30). In 1903-9 a million emigrated, and another million by 1914. The Church Emigration Society advertised in local magazines like the *Waxham and Happing Deanery Magazine*. Did any from Worstead use such schemes?

10. The relief of poverty

The Poor Law Amendment Act of 1834 laid down that the able-bodied poor were to receive help only by entering the workhouse, where living conditions were to be *'less eligible'* [a contemporary term meaning *'worse and therefore less likely to be chosen'*] than those of the poorest independent labourer. The aim was to reduce costs by ensuring that only the most destitute chose the workhouse. Despite the initial attractiveness of the workhouse as a way of disciplining the poor after the disturbances of the Swing Riots of 1830-31, the new policy ran counter to the custom of Norfolk Guardians, which was resumed in the mid 1840s, though they were careful to describe outdoor relief as *'against sickness'* which the New Poor Law allowed, not as *'against wages'* which it forbade. Sometimes applicants had to do the 'rounds' of local employers in the search for work, while others were employed in mending the roads and were paid out of rates collected by the parish Surveyors of Highways. The Tunstead and Happing Incorporation formally accepted the principles of the New Poor Law by 1837, though it did not legally become a Poor Law Union until 1869. It made minor amendments to the House of Industry at Smallburgh, which catered mostly for those of the aged, sick and orphans who could not look after themselves and for unmarried mothers (Norfolk's illegitimacy rate was 9-10% in the 1840s). Outdoor relief continued as the cheaper option for families, if not necessarily for single men, until the challenge of able-bodied pauperism had largely passed by the 1870s.

From its opening in 1785 to the abolition of workhouses in 1929, working people saw the Smallburgh House as a prison and felt stigmatised if they had to enter it. They ate better there than many workers outside; the sick received better medical attention than the Poor Law doctor provided outside; and the children were better educated than most outside, learning the four R's as well as 'industrial' skills. Inmates resented the uniform, the separation after 1834 of men from women and of adults from children, and the boring routine. Widows who lived outside were given very limited outdoor relief, maybe 1s.6d. or 2s. a week in the 1890s when the poverty line suggested they needed 4s.6d. Worstead people were involved in the running of the Incorporation and (after 1869) the Union: John Barnard was its Clerk in 1845 and Henry Riches Barnard its Assistant Clerk; by 1854 Henry was the sole Clerk (and also Registrar of Births, Marriages and Deaths). In 1902 Thomas Alfred Cross was the Assistant Overseer (the paid assistant to Worstead's Guardians) and George Ward was the Relieving Officer. In 1912 Austin Davison was the Assistant Overseer.

Worth £5.4s. a year in 1836, Themilthorpe's Charity was still giving a weekly loaf to twenty-five poor parishioners in 1912. The Parish Council, established under the Local Government Act of 1894, elected overseers to administer what was then called the Bread Charity. Like many Victorian parishes Worstead also had a Coal Charity, but when was it founded?

11. Named craftsmen and traders

Craftsmen and traders are listed in county directories, in census records, and less often in parish registers. Three issues of *White's Directory of Norfolk* in 1836, 1845 and 1854 give us a picture of the traders and craftsmen in the parish in the mid century together with the places where they were based. Some appear only once, but many three times.

Bengate
Miller: George Greenacre (at which mill?)
Shopkeepers: William Nash, Robert Tuck
Shoemaker: Jonathan Brackenbury

Briggate
Coal merchant: Joseph Tuck
Millers: John Balls, Christopher Sadler, Jonathan Roe

Brockley
Shopkeepers: Mary Weldon, William Woodrow

Lyngate
Shopkeeper: James Tooley

Meeting Hill
Bricklayer: John Lacey
Shoemaker: James Wright
Tailors: John Goose, William Swann (in Shalders' Yard by 1841)

Withergate
Gardener: William Blackbourne

Worstead Town

Shopkeepers: Elizabeth Barnard, William Cooper, Richard Marfrey,
Jacob Shalders, Walter Salisbury, Ann Tinker, Mary Watson,
Richard Watson, Miles Wiseman

Bakers: John Weasey Beane, Robert Cooper

Blacksmiths: John Sulley, Jeremiah Neave, Thomas Nelson, John Ducker

Bricklayer: Robert Steward, James Denham

Butchers: Richard Appleton, John Cross

Carrier: Henry Watts

Confectioner: John Spooner

Druggist: Charles Fromow (described as a chemist by 1854)

Glazier and painter: Robert Shipley

Joiner/carpenter: Robert Rump

Molecatcher: Zachariah Burrell

Postmistresses: Mary & Elizabeth Dyball

Postmaster: Jacob Shalders (by 1854)

Saddler: James Denham (also coffee shop in 1845), Jonathan Bowles

Shoemakers: Robert Ostler, Jonathan Roper, Jebediah Swann, Thomas
Wiseman

Tailors: Henry Watts, William Swann (by 1841)

Watchmaker: John Plummer

Wheelwrights: John Fryer, Richard Wenn

This list indicates that the non-farming economy of the parish centred on Worstead Town, though the mill and the canal at Briggate were also important. Some shops are identified (the baker, butchers, and so on), but what the eleven other shopkeepers sold is unspecified. A population of only 830 in 1831 probably could not provide a full livelihood for so many shopkeepers, and from the shopkeepers listed in 1836 only Jacob Shalders and Ann Tinker are described as such in the 1841 census, where William Nash, James Tooley, Robert Tuck, Mary Weldon, Miles Wiseman, William Woodrow and James Wright all appear as farmers. So their shops were evidently a sideline, probably selling farm produce.

A shorter list appears in *Kelly's Directory for Cambridgeshire, Norfolk & Suffolk* of 1883:

Shopkeepers: George Buck, William Cooper, John Slaughter, Mrs Jane
                Webster
Baker: Samuel Primrose Colman
Butchers: Miss Elizabeth Cross, Mrs Sarah Watson
Grocer & beer retailer in Meeting Hill: Robert Butcher
Grocer, draper & postmaster: James Benjamin Copping
Publicans: James Swan Burrell (the King's Head), William Cooper (the
                New Inn), William Hannant (the White Horse)
Tailor: Christmas Henry Watts
Shoemaker: Jebediah Swan
Blacksmiths: John Ducker, Robert Gibbs
Wheelwright: William Clark
Coal merchant, farmer & seedsman: Thomas Cross
Plumber, glazier & painter: John Starling
Thatcher: Robert Suffling
Carrier: James Rowe
Millers: Cubitt & Walker.

The list in *Kelly's Directory of Norfolk* in 1912 is even shorter:

Grocer, draper and postmaster: James Benjamin Copping
Butchers: Robert Amies, Austin Davison, George Norgate
Baker: Samuel Grimes
Publicans: Lewis Bailey (the White Horse), Mary Colman (the New Inn),
                George Pyecroft (the King's Head)
Blacksmith: Henry Forder
Carpenter: Mrs Isaac Fiddy
Bricklayer: David Blower
Decorator: William C Colman
Shoemaker: James Grimes

Tailor: Christmas Henry Watts
Coal merchant: George Hill
Miller: Cubitt & Walker
Carrier: James S Burrell
Insurance agent: Henry E Cooper

All the craftsmen listed are male, except for Mrs Isaac Fiddy who appears as a carpenter in 1912. Fewer women than men participated in commerce, for example two postmistresses and three shopkeepers in 1836, and two butchers in 1883. Two female landladies were licensed at the White Horse in the nineteenth century but no landladies appear at the other named public houses until the twentieth century. The censuses record women as teachers, governesses, nursemaids, nurses, seamstresses, dressmakers, housekeepers, charwomen, washerwomen, dairymaids, housemaids, and servants. Many servants, most of them female and often young, lived in. Few of the larger houses could function without them; and as late as the 1920s Holly Grove House (*21*) had four live-in servants.

Fig 109 Christmas Henry Watts outside Haggar House, his shop. Courtesy Mr B Hedge

Those listed as tailors in the directories are all male. Henry Watts is listed as a tailor in 1841 and 1861 and as a tailor, grocer and draper in 1871 in

Haggar House (9) in Back Street. Christmas Henry Watts, born in Swanton Abbot, was already, aged 22, a tailor in 1871 but is then recorded as a visitor alongside Henry in Back Street. By 1883 *Kelly's Directory* names Christmas Henry as a tailor and shopkeeper, which he still was in 1912. The first floor workroom at the southern end of the seventeenth/eighteenth Haggar House has a large window close to the floor, before which he sat cross-legged tailoring worsted suits, from cloth probably woven in Yorkshire. Vestiges of the shop front are visible at the northern end of the frontage and the shop's internal fittings are now in Gressenhall Museum. Other tailors worked in the parish:

John Goose in Meeting Hill (1836)
William Swann in Meeting Hill (1836) and in Shalders Yard (1841, 1861)
William Howard in Briggate (1841, 1861)
Henry Harrison in Shalders Yard (1841)
Frederick Christmas (1871).

However the censuses of 1841, 1861 and 1871 record twenty-one female dressmakers or seamstresses, as against seven male tailors:

In 1841: Ann Tinker
   Ann Rump
   Jane Shalders

In 1841 and 1861: Frances Sizer

In 1861: Harriet and Charlotte Grimes
   Elizabeth Long
   Mary Ann Howard
   Mary Ann Brackenbury
   Elizabeth Goodson
   Jemima Potter,
   Charlotte Kirk,
   Mary Watts (daughter of Henry)
   Maria Clarke

In 1861 and 1871: Elizabeth Hannant
   Clara Thorsby

In 1871: Mary Gown
        Mary Self
        Sarah Turner
        Maria Hannant
        Ann Wiseman

Mary Gown and Mary Self described themselves as tailoresses.

In the running of the Post Office women just outnumber men. The churchwardens' accounts, which start in 1737, first record the paying of postage on a letter in 1796. If the payment was made at a post office, as seems likely because the Penny Black was the first stamp in 1840, it may have been in Honing Row, where Mary and Elizabeth Dyball were postmistresses in 1836. In 1796 Elizabeth was about 30. She was 75 in 1841 when she was still postmistress. Mary, then aged 74, was named as postmistress in 1845. In 1836 letters were received at 11.00 am and despatched at 3.00 pm. By 1854 the post office was sited in Jacob Shalders' Norwich House Stores, where letters were received at 9.00 am and despatched at 3.30 pm. Jacob died in 1857 and Mary Cross was recorded as the postmistress in Back Street in 1861 and 1871. By 1883 - and still in 1912 - James Benjamin Copping ran the post office alongside his grocery and drapery in Norwich House Stores.

12. A revolution in transport

Early in Victoria's reign people travelled on foot, on horseback or in a horse-drawn conveyance, while goods were carried mostly by cart. There were coaches or carriages in the parish, Robert Leader appears as a coachman in 1841, George Woolnough in 1861 and George Woolner in 1871. The two Georges lived at the same address: which was the correct spelling of their surname? The North Walsham carrier (Robert Coe in 1845) departed for Yarmouth on Tuesdays and Fridays at 8.30 am, but Worstead had its own carrier who journeyed to Norwich on Saturdays: Henry Watts is recorded as the carrier in 1836, 1845 and 1854; Thomas Balls in 1841; James Rowe in 1861, 1871 and 1883; James S Burrell in 1904. In 1854 an omnibus ran from the New Inn to Norwich at 8.00 am on Saturdays. The coming of the railways was the death knell of turnpikes: the road to Norwich ceased to be a turnpike in 1873, just a year before the railway reached Worstead, and was adopted by Norfolk County Council soon after it came into being in 1888-89.

Motor vehicles were seen in Worstead before World War I. May Kershaw, the Vicar's daughter, recalled that as a six year old in 1912 she ran into a shop in fright when she first saw a car in the village. George Smith said that the first car owner in Worstead was Mr Cross, perhaps the Robert Tuck Cross who gave £50 towards the cost of the war memorial. Joshua Unwin, who married Emma Louise Woodhouse in 1912 and lived at Meeting Hill, was employed as a chauffeur before World War I, but was killed in 1915. By the 1930s there was enough motor traffic to support Austin Davison's garage, which was on the sites now occupied by Cherry Tree Cottage in Front Street and the timber-clad building called the Barn opposite.

Fig 110 'Gongoozlers' watching a wherry pass through Briggate Lock Early C20.
Image Courtesy – North Walsham and Dilham Canal Trust

Some Worstead people worked on the North Walsham and Dilham Canal. The census records John Brackenbury of Briggate as a waterman in 1841, 1861 and 1871, and he was joined by his sons Charles and Alfred in 1871. George and Lowell Roper of Meeting Hill appear as boatmen in 1861 but Lowell alone in 1871. In 1871 James Bates and his son James (both of Meeting Hill) and George Harmer and Alfred Hewitt (both of Worstead) are all described as watermen. Perhaps they were among those canal workers who took liquid refreshment at the White Horse in Briggate. If so, their custom did not provide the landlord with a living wage. William Hannant, who kept the pub between 1856 and 1883, needed a second job: he was a shoemaker in the census of 1861 and a farmer of seven acres in 1881. Did watermen and wherrymen keep Robert Butcher, the grocer and beer retailer of Meeting Hill, in business? Did he run the unidentified beer house that was sold in 1899 and had its licence transferred to the Duke of Edinburgh Public House in Bacton? Despite its Baptist connections and its branch of the teetotal Band of Hope, Meeting Hill would probably have offered alcoholic refreshment to those who loaded and unloaded wherries at the Meeting House Staithe.

Fig 111 Repairs to the breach at Bacton Wood 1912.
Image Courtesy – North Walsham and Dilham Canal Trust

The canal tolls, collected at Tonnage Bridge just north of Dilham, began quite high, but were reduced by 1844, so that coal, corn and flour were charged at 3d. per ton per mile. Even then, it proved cheaper to beach collier ships at Mundesley or at Bacton Green's Cable Gap and to cart the coal from there, at least until 1874 when the railway reached Worstead from Norwich. So, deprived of a good revenue from coal, this late-comer to the canal era was not a commercial success: receipts averaged £360 a year in 1826-44. Traffic on the canal may also have been slowed by a lack of water to operate the locks. So in 1886 the Canal Company sold the canal for £600 to Edward Press, who farmed at Spa Common and was a partner in Press Brothers: sadly the chief clerk, James Turner, absconded with most of the funds. The Press Brothers owned Ebridge Mill and a fleet of at least seven trading wherries, which were converted in the summer to pleasure 'wherry-yachts.' In 1893 the upper 1.4 miles of the canal above Swafield were abandoned, but the rest of the canal remained operational. In 1906, when Edward Press died, the canal was sold at auction for £2250 to a London company. In the Great Flood of 26-27 August 1912 seven and a half inches of rain fell in twenty-nine hours: the canal bank was breached above Bacton Wood, and several staithes and all the locks were badly damaged.

Fig 112 Worstead Station drawn by Mike McEwen ©Worstead Parish Council

The twin tracks of the East Norfolk Railway's line from Norwich to North Walsham opened on 20 October 1874. The line was run by the Great Eastern Railway from the start and later came into the GER's ownership. It was extended to Cromer in 1877. Worstead Station was in the hamlet of Brockley. It had two platforms. Wooden buildings on the down side were the original ticket office and waiting rooms, but they have not survived. The brick buildings on the up side were later Great Eastern Railway additions and they survive, at present unused. There was a goods yard on the up side with sidings which have left traces, but it was closed on 13 July 1964. The wooden signal box remains but no longer functions. The level crossing gates, now replaced by automatic barriers, were huge, requiring substantial diagonal bracing from tall posts. In the 1890s twelve or fourteen trains a day left Norwich but two terminated at Wroxham and three or four did not stop at Worstead. The two staff houses still exist. The station master in 1883 was Frederick William Avery, whose successor Charles Wilby was in office by 1923. Local people employed by the railway included signalman G Allard, signalman E Grimes and porter-signalman Henry Baldry, who was injured by a tow rope in 1911. In 1912 coal merchant George Hill was based in the station yard. In the Edwardian era the Great Eastern Railway ran non-stop expresses from London to North Walsham via the Wensum Curve in Norwich, thus avoiding Thorpe Station. Imagine steam-powered expresses thundering through Worstead.

The Eastern and Midlands Railway from North Walsham to Stalham opened in 1879-80, but came into the ownership of the Midland and Great Northern Joint Railway after its formation in 1893. Honing for Worstead Station (*26 - NHER 13581*) lay just over the North Walsham and Dilham Canal from Briggate. There are still visible remains of this impressive station, and the signal box is now at Barton House Railway, Wroxham. In the 1890s there were four or five trains a day between North Walsham Town and Yarmouth Beach in each direction, but only one or two made a scheduled stop at Honing for Worstead, though a further one or two trains could be requested to stop. The line was not a great commercial success and it closed in 1959.

Fig 113 One of the town centre's listed buildings. K6 telephone box designed by Sir Giles Gilbert Scott in 1935.

6. WORSTEAD IN THE TWENTIETH CENTURY

1. Living and working in and between the World Wars

Worstead was directly involved in World War I because many of its men went to the front, leaving behind anxious mothers and fathers, wives and children, and sweethearts. Some did not return: their roles and their fates are covered by Steve Smith (2012).

Fig 114 World War I & World War II memorials

Worstead itself suffered relatively little damage. May Kershaw, the Vicar's daughter, who spoke of her terror at first seeing an aeroplane in 1913, soon - from January 1915 - became used to German zeppelins flying above on their way to bomb Norwich, one dropping incendiary bombs near the station. A zeppelin in trouble in 1918 off-loaded its bombs near Briggate Mill, causing the chimney for the steam engine to list to one side. May Kershaw also became accustomed to aeroplanes, because Boulton & Paul made some 2,530 planes on the airfield on Mousehold Heath.

Farmers were deprived of labour, as workers volunteered for war service or were conscripted from early 1916. Six farm workers from the parish were killed: Thomas Self of Meeting Hill at Gallipoli in 1915; John Henry Roper and Herbert John Cooper, both of Briggate, at the Somme in 1916; George Sidney Sidell, of Station Road, at the second Battle of the Scarpe in 1917; and Frederick Delf and Charles George Rump, both of Meeting Hill, in minor actions in June 1918. Farmers were also deprived of motive power because many horses and donkeys were commandeered for military use. With many men absent at the front, women stepped into jobs once regarded as male, many in the manufacture of munitions, others in the Women's Land Army. The Land Army registered more than 5,000 female farm workers in Norfolk, but at least as many women worked on the land unregistered. Worstead women and children not employed in war service raised funds and made dressings and other items for men at the front.

For lack of men and horses, agricultural production fell at a time when U-boat attacks were disrupting the import of foreign foodstuffs. The government took action. Some 6,000 Fordson tractors were ordered from the United States of America, but when did the first tractor arrive in Worstead? Horses evidently remained the chief motive power: Manor Farm, owned by the Newton family in the 1920s, kept some thirty-five horses in the charge of head horseman Dan Chapman. It still had a dozen tumbrils (horse-drawn tipping carts) in 1950 and twenty-two horses in 1955. The War Agricultural Committee for Norfolk established allotments to increase the food supply and the press carried advice on how to make less food go further. Until 1917 the government tried to control food supply by fixing maximum prices, so that everyone could afford to buy food. In 1917 a voluntary rationing scheme was introduced, but rationing for meats and fats became compulsory in 1918.

The war exposed how poor were the nation's health and housing: only 58.5% of recruits for the armed forces were found fit for active service; only 56.9% in Norfolk. Despite the Liberals' reforms before the war, it became evident that children in school were still under-nourished and ill-clothed. There was also a wide perception that those who made sacrifices in wartime deserved to have their say in government. So in 1918 the wartime coalition government was re-elected on a new franchise which gave men over 21 and women over 30 the vote (women over

21 got the vote in 1928). In 1918 the school-leaving age was raised from twelve to fourteen: at Worstead School, then an all-age elementary school, the headmaster Thomas H Ford was a stern disciplinarian in the 1920s and 1930s. In 1919 the Housing Act planned to fulfil the 1918 election promise of 500,000 *Homes fit for Heroes* within three years. Mile Cross in Norwich was among the first council estates, and Worstead Parish Council often discussed the building of council housing between 1918 and 1930: such housing can be seen in several locations across the parish. Unemployment insurance, which had covered 2,250,000 men in 1914, was extended to 12,000,000 in 1920.

The men returning from the war entered the labour market just as wartime production ceased. So the 1920s began in economic difficulty and industrial unrest which brought the General Strike in 1926. Life and work became much harder when in 1929 the Wall Street Crash ushered in a long depression. Farmers suffered from low and fluctuating corn prices, and low labourers' wages had to be supplemented by wives and children, who picked fruit at the Westwick fruit farm, helped employed farm workers earn their harvest wage of £11, and gleaned the post-harvest fields.

Fig 115 Part of the War Memorial display

A picture of farming between the wars emerges from notes made by a former inhabitant of Bengate Farm *(23)*. The now splendid farmhouse was then the centre of a workaday farm. The kitchen was its heart: it had a stove-blacked range and a wall-oven; a slate sink, a copper in the corner, and an indoor water pump; a floor paved with uneven red pamments; a well-scrubbed table in the centre; a large walk-in pantry, with homemade beer and wine standing on the cold floor and sometimes popping corks; and mice a-plenty! The dairy was at the back of the house, with its hand-cranked butter churn and butter pats. Bengate Farm was a mixed farm, as many Worstead farms must have been. The corn was probably harvested by a horse-drawn reaper-binder, threshed by a steam-driven threshing machine, and carried in sacks by horse and cart to Briggate Mill. The horses did all the work of the farm: they were fed in the stable on chaff and chopped swedes and were watered at the farmyard pit. Stabled in winter, they were on summer nights turned out to graze, perhaps - once the hay was cut - on the meadow beyond the Midland and Great Northern Railway that ran from North Walsham Town to Honing for Worstead (*26*) and beyond. Bullocks were fattened on cattle cake and mangold-wurzels which were ground by hand-cranked machines in the barn; pigs were fed scraps from the kitchen; and geese and hens scratched round the farmyard.

Fig 116 Bengate Farm Drawn by Mike McEwen ©Worstead Parish Council

Some of Bengate Farm's fields were called the Top Piece, Fuzz (probably Furze) Hill and the Pyghtle. George Smith recalled other field names from the 1920s and 1930s (I Rendall 2000): Barks and Simms, Dusty Sheds, Hall Pieces, Fair Piece, Patch Loke, Fourteen Acres, Widdly Pits, and Ammunition Piece. The last took its name from the Militia's

Ammunition House: it stood north of the Westwick Road as it leaves Worstead until its closure in 1814 and was drawn by John Starling before it disappeared. Some of these field names may still be used in the small farming community, but not by most villagers who now have little contact with farming. The origins of some names are clear: Obelisk Field was named after the eighteenth century folly (*31*) just beyond the western parish boundary. Ollands, which survives in house names at the top of Swann's Yard, derives from *old land* or *arable left unused.* Other field names, before and after enclosure, are recorded by K I Sandred (1996).

Lieutenant-Colonel Rous died on 12 April 1914, aged 80, and the Worstead Estate passed to a minor, the Hon. William Keith Rous, the second son of the third Earl of Stradbroke (he became the fifth Earl for a few days before his death in 1983). In 1938 the estate was acquired by Sir Harold Harmsworth. He demolished Worstead House in 1939: it was never rebuilt, but the stables survive, listed grade II because they are a rare Norfolk example of the work of the architect James Wyatt (1746-1813).

World War II came nearer to Worstead than World War I: there were fewer casualties on the battlefield, but more close to home. East Anglia was targeted because it was full of airfields used by the Royal Air Force from 1939 and by the United States Army Air Force (USAAF) from 1942. Bombing was a real hazard: bombs fell on Withergate and Philpot's Farm in June 1940 and on Meeting Hill in October: eighty panes of frosted glass show the extent of bomb damage to the chapel. Bombs killed three in Scottow in August 1940 and one in Worstead in February 1941. Air raids faded out in 1943, leaving 322 dead in Norwich, others in Great Yarmouth and King's Lynn, and eight in rural Norfolk. There was sadness when 'our' planes crashed: two from RAF Coltishall came down in the parish in 1941, a Hurricane at Duffields Farm in April and a Beaufighter in Worstead Park in May; and a Spitfire from another RAF station crashed in '*that lane that leads down to Mr Swan's*' Swan Cottage (*39* - NHER 47795). Norfolk was seen as a likely target for a German invasion. A twenty mile defence zone, from which all visitors were excluded, was declared in June 1940, but reduced to five miles in December. The North Walsham and Dilham Canal had changed hands in 1921, coming into the ownership of the North Walsham Canal Company, which still exists. Wherries could then still reach Briggate and Bacton Wood, but the last trading voyage was made in December 1934 by the wherry *Ella*, itself the last trading wherry to be built at Allen's Yard in Coltishall in 1912. The canal closed in 1935, but it now became part of the defences. It was deepened to create a serious obstacle for tanks (NHER 45233) and pillboxes were built: four still survive in the parish, three near Briggate Bridge (NHER 21553, 32561, 17019) and one in Meeting Hill (NHER 18036). There were also two gun emplacements on Sandy Hill overlooking the Ant Valley. Briggate Mill lost its water-wheel in about 1943 and after World War II was driven by electricity. Closed in 1969, it was badly damaged by fire in an arson attack in 1975, which led to charges of conspiracy, arson and insurance fraud and to a long court case. Its ruins were demolished in 2012.

Fig 117 World War II pillbox – one of four remaining in the parish

From 1941 women were conscripted into the ATS, the WRENS and the WAAF (though not in combat roles), into Civil Defence and the Women's Land Army, into munitions, nursing and other essential work. Those at home in Worstead received their share of evacuees or had soldiers billeted upon them from May 1941, when a large training camp (NHER 34541) was opened in Worstead Park. Many women who were not conscripted joined the Women's Voluntary Service (WVS - later the WRVS) or worked to sew items to help the war effort at the Red Cross and Women's Institute: both organisations were active in Worstead. Shortages were common: petrol (soon rationed for essential uses only), clothes (rationed from June 1941), furniture, even paper and pencils. People became used to *Utility* brands which tried to do more with less. The greatest shortage was food, as foreign supplies were severely restricted by submarine warfare. Land girls, like the late Elsie Hudson (latterly an inhabitant of Max Carter Close), helped the farm labour shortage. There were 1650 land girls in Norfolk by 1944, but they made up only 25% of the women who worked on the land. The Dig for Victory campaign enabled the Norfolk War Executive Committee to seek out sites for allotments, including in Worstead. Rationing, not only for food, began in January 1940. Beer, weakened and expensive, and bread were not rationed, but the white loaf which used only 70% of the wheat grain became the 'National Wholemeal Loaf' which used 85%. The change was not popular!

The memorial to those who fell in the First World War was dedicated on 20.6.1920. The Vicar, the Rev Charles William Kershaw, and the Church-wardens, Edmund Waters and Miss Maud E Chettleburgh, submitted an application for a faculty to erect a war memorial in St Mary's, but the prime movers seem to have been Robert Tuck Cross, who gave £50 towards its cost, and Mr G Buck. Annual Armistice Day Services were held from 1921, when about eighty veterans paraded, led by Lieutenant Colonel A H Besant, tenant of Holly Grove House and its farm, aided by Sergeant Major Dick Downie of Briggate. The names of those who fell in the Second World War were added to the memorial and the second part of it was dedicated on 6th November 1949. A separate memorial tablet records the death in action in September 1943 of Captain Charles Hugh Monk Kershaw, the son of the Vicar. The Rev C W Kershaw left Worstead for Bacton in October 1943 after thirty-one years.

2. Attempts to revive worsted weaving in Worstead

In 1851 the Great Exhibition at Crystal Palace expressed British confidence in the machine age, but some - notably John Ruskin - argued that machines destroyed people's creativity and quality of life. Ruskin's ideas were taken up by William Morris and members of the Pre-Raphelite Movement, a group of artists dedicated to achieving medieval forms using medieval skills. Their work led to the Arts and Crafts Movement. From 1861 the firm of Morris, Marshall, Faulkener and Company, Fine Art Workmen, used traditional craft skills to produce work of high quality. Morris was a keen weaver and his floral designs are still popular. But few could afford hand-woven fabric, and the revival of hand loom weaving in the later nineteenth century was not a commercial success. Even so, Ethel Mairet set up an apprentice system in her home at Ditchling in Sussex in 1920. Elizabeth Peacock established a weaving workshop nearby and with Mabel Dawson founded the Guild of Weavers, Spinners and Dyers. From there the craft revival gathered pace, reaching Worstead in 1949.

In 1944 all state education was made free and the primary sector was introduced for ages five to eleven and the secondary sector for ages eleven to fifteen. Worstead School became a primary school. Its headmaster, Henry Wright, learned weaving one summer at the London School of Weaving and proposed to teach it to his pupils in school time and to adults at evening classes. He persuaded the International Wool Secretariat to present to the school a loom made by Miss Dorothy Wilkinson, Principal of the London School of Weaving. Mr Wright said the occasion was historic because it revived...

the ancient industry of weaving worsted cloth in its name-place... [and is] a means of teaching a child, who is not capable of being taught through his head, through his hands.

At the presentation on 1st November 1949, Mr Ewen Waterman, the Australian member of the International Wool Secretariat, welcomed the school's initiative, saying '*Worsted from Worstead can become a reality again.*' He used a stamp of Worstead's coat-of-arms to certify a piece of blue worsted suiting woven by Mr Wright and Miss Wilkinson. It was later sent to US President Harry Truman. The occasion was filmed by the BBC: was this Worstead's first appearance on television?

Fig 118 Nameplate of Johnstons Weavers

In the same week as the presentation Mr and Mrs J R S Johnston moved into White Cottage *(14, - NHER 50420)*. They set up two looms in a shed at the top of the present garden, establishing Worstead Hand Loom Weavers with the aim of restarting the commercial production of hand-woven fabric. Their enterprise failed by 1952. However they bequeathed to the cottage their company nameplate, a sheet of their headed notepaper, and some loose-weave furnishing fabric. Two mid twentieth century postcards call White Cottage a weaver's cottage: this was true in 1949-52 but probably not earlier.

Henry Wright remained at the school until 1971, teaching weaving to pupils and adults. Spinning and weaving was demonstrated at the Worstead Festival from 1966. In 1972 Mrs Maltman and Mrs Morris of the Norfolk and Suffolk Guild of Weavers, Spinners and Dyers helped Worstead to start its own Guild, with seventeen founder members, among them Thelma Richards who taught at the school in 1961-88. Mrs Morris taught the Guild until 1977. The new Guild took its name from St Mary's, because the Rev Donald Pettit offered its members space for their looms in the north aisle of the church. They wove cloth for the church's furnishings: the frontal and altar-piece in the Chapel of St John the Baptist were major projects, and other work included curtains, kneelers and cushions.

Fig 119 Altarpiece by the Worstead Guild of Weavers, Spinners and Dyers.

3. The closure of the Methodist Chapel

The reunion of the major denominations within Methodism in 1932 left the newly reunited Methodist Church with too many chapels. Worstead's Chapel soldiered on: Ethel Chapman's Second World War diary records her attendance at both the Chapel and at St Mary's and mentions various inter-denominational services. But the Chapel closed in the early 1960s: its records end in 1962. The building reverted to the ownership of Norwich House and is now a holiday cottage.

4. Saving St Mary's and the Worstead Festival

In 1965 the report of the Diocesan Architect on St Mary's Church was most disturbing: there were huge cracks in the tower; death-watch beetle in the roof-timbers, and serious damp problems. The repairs were costed at £36,000, a sum beyond the normal fundraising efforts of the congregation. The Vicar, the Rev Joscelyn Fellowes-Brown, challenged the people of Worstead to '*Work with us to save the Church.*' The result was the first Worstead Festival, held on 29-31 July 1966. It enabled £13,000 to be spent on essential work by the time of the second Festival in 1967.

Fig 120 The Queen Mother's steps. She visited St Mary's in 1985

The tower was saved from collapse, but lost its four pinnacles. They had been added to the tower in 1861, to the disgust of Walter Rye, who described them as *'hideous, modern and tulip-like.'* They survived a restoration of the tower in 1908 (at the cost of £800), but had to be removed in 1966 after lightning damage. Two of the bells were recast in 1970 by the Whitechapel Bell Foundry and all the bells were re-hung on steel girders. Even the restored tower was not strong enough for change ringing and the bells are now rung as a carillon. Further restoration included the tackling of the damp and the death-watch beetle, and the removal of the nineteenth century varnish from the rood screen and the fixing of the medieval paint. St Mary's was indeed saved, although defects in its fabric are once again becoming evident. In 1979 St Mary's celebrated 600 years since the rebuilding that began in 1379. To commemorate this anniversary Anton Wagner, a refugee from Nazi Austria in 1938 who lived and worked in the village, carved a wooden image of the Virgin of the Annunciation. It stands north of the altar in the Lady Chapel. Another of Anton's carvings, an image of St Nicholas, graces the centre aisle.

Fig 121 The Virgin of the Annunciation by Anton Wagner

7. WORSTEAD IN WHITE COTTAGE

White Cottage, first painted white and named as late as 1949, is one of Worstead's less grand houses, but its story - interesting in itself - casts some light on the wider history of the parish. Margaret and I bought it in 1999, knowing that it needed restoration, including re-roofing. Our aim was to conserve as much as we could both of the original cottage and of its alterations through time: the way old buildings grow and develop is a fascinating part of their history.

Fig 122 White Cottage 2015

As we planned the restoration we sought the advice of the local authority's planning department, although none of the work we proposed needed planning permission. We wanted to understand a little about the building and its construction and the Conservation Officer offered some useful advice, notably, that injecting a damp-proof course (dpc) into the cottage's solid brick walls built on a cobble foundation would be ineffective and probably harmful. We consulted Norfolk building archaeologist Edwin Rose, who visited the cottage. His report (NHER 50420) gave us some insights and at the time we accepted his conclusion that the cottage started out as a single storey L-shaped building. However a recent detailed survey, conducted by Stefan Ganther with the kind permission of Andrew and Wendy Millar (the present owners), suggests a different story.

This chapter seeks to explain how some of the architectural history of White Cottage has been uncovered, in the hope that other Worstead folk may be enthused to explore the architecture of their own dwelling and to investigate how their property fits into the jigsaw that is the history of Worstead. In our own exploration we were helped by the deeds which refer back to the later eighteenth century. They provide good evidence about the cottage's owners, but much less about its occupants. So there is further research to do in the manorial rolls, the parish registers from 1558, the civil registers from 1837, and the censuses which from 1841 tell us who lived where and their ages and employments. The Norfolk Record Office is a fine resource and the archivists there are willing to advise on people and property searches. Its catalogues are 'on-line' and so it is easy to find out whether there are sources that are relevant to one's research. The Enclosure and Tithe maps (available on-line at Norfolk E-Map Explorer) make a good starting point. The Record Office holds the originals of these maps and other records associated with them. The maps identify the owners of land and property and seem to distinguish between those buildings that are residential and those that are not.

1. Location

The present cottage lies on the west side of Front Street. To the north and physically connected lies Jean's Cottage, an eighteenth century dwelling, and beyond that the White Lady (formerly the New Inn). The long garden of White Cottage shares its northern boundary with the White Lady: the dividing wall, built mainly of later seventeenth century brick, is listed with the pub and is in need of conservation. To the south the cottage is flanked by Cherry Tree Cottage, which replaced the village garage in the later twentieth century (the garage - certainly active from the 1920s - also used the timber clad building, now The Barn, on the opposite side of Front Street next to Clemsea House). The cottage garden also shares half of its southern boundary with Max Carter Close.

Fig 123 Map 1827
NRO ref C/Sca2/342

Fig 124 Map Today
Courtesy Historic England

The 1827 map above shows a building to the west of the cottage extending beyond its southern boundary. It does not appear on earlier maps and vanishes from later maps after 1906, and no traces of it survive. Owned by Sir George Berney Brograve, its different hatching on the map indicates a non-residential use.

The maps show that the present garden did not belong to the cottage in 1827. When the site of Sir George Berney Brograve's building came into the possession of the cottage is unclear. Possibly the transfer of ownership occurred when the 'lower part' of the garden was purchased in 1949 by Mabel Hunn: she paid £35 to Sir Harold Harmsworth, then owner of the Worstead Estate, for part of plot 121 on the 1906 Ordnance Survey map.

In the seventeenth century the site on which White Cottage now stands fronted onto the original market place, which occupied the space between Front and Back Streets and was devoid of permanent structures until the market moved to North Walsham in 1666. The importance of the link between the site and the market will become clearer as the story of the site unfolds.

2. Archaeology

The archaeological finds made in the centre of Worstead are noted in Chapter 1 but they cast little light on the history of White Cottage. No formal archaeological excavation has been undertaken on the site, and so few early finds have been made: a Stone Age scraper; a sherd or two of later medieval pottery; many oyster shells, more probably enjoyed by medieval people than by Romans; pieces of dressed limestone from the rebuilding of St Mary's from the late fourteenth to the early sixteenth century or from the demolition of St Andrews in the mid sixteenth century, eight reused in the wall between the cottage and the pub, and one found in the floor of the ingle-nook fireplace in the northern gable wall; and two knapped facing flints which may have strayed from the flushwork of St Mary's exterior or been simply discarded by on-site flint knappers.

Fig 125 The shoe and quern stone – where they were found.

The cultivation levels in the garden close to the cottage have yielded finds from the eighteenth to the twentieth century. Only one gives us a reasonably precise date: the date on a very worn George II halfpenny found in the garden is illegible but its 'old head' was used between 1740 and 1754. Much of the pottery is of little significance and of no great age. Some sherds are copies of the blue and white willow pattern imported from China in the eighteenth century. Others are plain or patterned china tableware of the nineteenth or twentieth century. Some brown- or cream-glazed earthenware and grey- or white-glazed stoneware, was thrown on a wheel and may date from the nineteenth century, but more was made in a mould, such as an early twentieth century marmalade jar. The brown earthenware includes part of an old kitchen sink. There was much bottle glass, but few bottle stoppers: one screw top, made from a composite material in the nineteenth century, bears the name of Jones and Crawshay of Norwich. Among the many pieces of clay pipe were no complete bowls, and only one stem bears a maker's name, Fitt. A glass ashtray of mid twentieth century date is inscribed

'Senior Service' - then a popular brand of cigarette. Toys found include a badly-damaged lead elephant, hollow-cast in the later nineteenth century; three marbles, made from marble, not glass, probably in the nineteenth century; an early model of a penny-farthing bicycle made of a composite material, and the roller from a toy steam-roller, made by Britain's Ltd in the mid twentieth century. To what early car did a wheel-nut belong? And what soldier, perhaps on leave, dropped the standard issue military button of World War I from his greatcoat? The archaeology leaves us with more questions than answers.

Many different building materials came to light during the restoration of the cottage. Some hard flooring bricks still lay directly on the earth and a few showed the wear characteristic of a threshold. Fragments of pantiles were common. The earliest window glass found has a pale green tint and was handmade with a rolled edge. Some thicker dark green glass may have come from some Victorian stained glass: a reused leaded window in clear glass gives a view of the front door from the kitchen. Much of the ironwork found was forged by blacksmiths, probably locally: cupboard and door hinges, door latches, window fastenings, a window bar, and various types of nails.

Beneath the kitchen floor - taken up because it sounded hollow - we uncovered the remains of a brick-built, barrel-vaulted undercroft, labelled (1) on the plan below. It was possible to see that the springing of the vault on the north side continued under the present stairs, perhaps as far as the broken brick ends which evidence the removal of an earlier wall (3). This vaulted undercroft will be discussed below.

In the back wall of the ingle-nook fireplace was a hook which once supported the apparatus that held a pot over the fire. Across the chimney opening was a 'nightmare' bar: it testified to the superstition that a nightmare coming down the chimney would hit the bar, rattle the ring on it, and flee whence it came! Both the hook and the bar have recently been removed to permit the installation of a log-burning stove. Superstition may also explain the probably nineteenth century shoe and the quern stone (4) that we found carefully placed the right way up beneath the concrete floor near the present step up into the kitchen. It may also account for the unwelcome mummified rat found in the loft!

3. Architecture

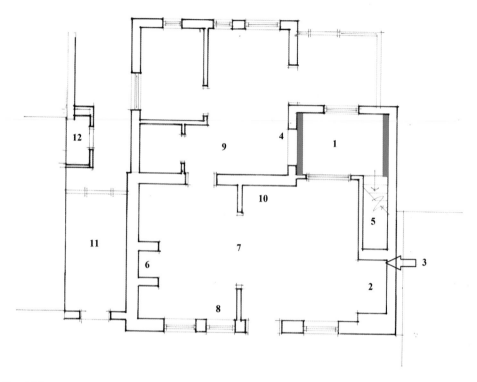

Fig 126

KEY

1 = the undercroft beneath the present kitchen
2 = the ingle-nook fireplace and chimney
3 = broken brick ends evidence the removal of an earlier wall
4 = the site of the buried shoe and worn quern stone
5 = the present staircase
6 = the second fireplace and chimney
7 = the partition wall
8 = the door opening into the smaller half of the divided cottage
9 = the outshut building
10 = the possible location of earlier stairs
11 = the covered passageway that served as James Grimes' shop
12 = the nineteenth century privy
■ *= Known extent of vaulting*

Fig 127 Rear view of White Cottage

When Margaret and I first viewed White Cottage in late 1998, I noticed that the old knocker on its squat early nineteenth century door consisted of a small bust of Admiral Lord Nelson. It resembles a full-size bust now held by Paston Sixth Form College (Nelson was a pupil at the Paston School in 1769-71). Such memorabilia were popular in the years after his death at the battle of Trafalgar in 1805 and the knocker was later removed for safety. I discovered later that the parish has another connection with Nelson: John Starr or Starling, who drew the sixteenth century house (demolished in the nineteenth century) on Church Plain, was present on the quarter-deck of the Victory when Nelson was killed in 1805.

Betty Marples welcomed us and quickly drew our attention to the black-painted beam above a 1930s fireplace which then projected into the room. The beam - or, more correctly, the bressumer - suggested that an ingle-nook fireplace (2) had been filled in. It was inscribed with the date of 1617 in Jacobean script. The removal of the 1930s fireplace did reveal a large ingle-nook, unlock some of its secrets and pose further questions. After shifting huge amounts of rubble we found that the north gable wall was constructed in early post-medieval brick, no later than the early to mid seventeenth century. The left hand return (the side wall) of the ingle-nook (2) is built in bricks that carry the diagonal markings or scintlings characteristic of later seventeenth century brick-making. It is not tied into the back wall of the fireplace, so it is an insertion within an older building, because the back wall shows broken ends of bricks where a structure was removed from a slightly different alignment (3). More probably the broken brick ends are evidence of the removal of an earlier wall, one that belonged to the building that first housed the undercroft and most probably the oldest part of the building. On the right side of the fireplace, the bressumer was let only a few inches into the soft Norfolk brick of the front wall, not far enough - said our experienced builder Ivan Farrow - to carry the huge weight of the chimney stack. So he built a new right hand return from reclaimed bricks, many from the rubble we had removed.

Fig 128 & 129 Details from the bressumer

What did the date of 1617 on the bressumer signify? It is unlikely to be the date on which the beam became the bressumer, because the brickwork evidence indicates that the chimney was not built before the later seventeenth century. Did the date have a special significance for the person who built the chimney? Or was the beam recycled from another structure? Was that structure the one that contained the undercroft? If so, did it date from 1617 or was it already in existence? Or did the beam come from another building entirely? The structure of White Cottage has experienced many changes and adaptations, not least the bressumer itself. We lack all the evidence we need and - as so often - we are left with frustrating unknowns and can only make an educated guess at how things developed. At a later stage (and most likely in the Georgian period) the bressumer was hacked to key a plaster covering, but the chisel marks avoid a crude graffito of a church tower or windmill and the incised initials F Y, which remain unidentified. Then, perhaps in Edwardian times, it and all the other beams were painted black, but we restored them to their original natural colour.

Although the building archaeologist Edwin Rose was aware of the undercroft, he interpreted it as a cheese vault that was integral to the original 'L' shaped footprint of the dwelling. Because of his advice we did not investigate further, but in hindsight we should have at least attempted to discover the full extent of the vaulted structure: how far did its floor lie below the present kitchen floor; how - in detail - was it constructed? What we did see was that the vault sprang out of the side walls of the present kitchen (1). This surviving physical evidence indicates that the brick-built barrel-vault structure was a substantial undercroft (shown in green outline on the plan) and that it belongs to the first phase of the building that became White Cottage.

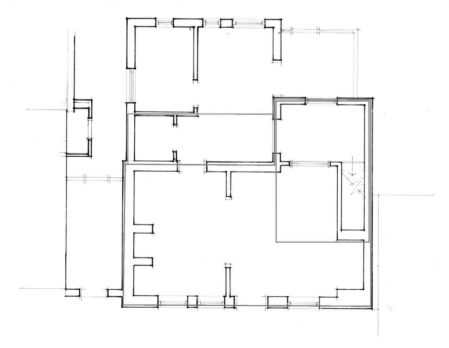

Fig 130 Ground floor plan showing phases of construction

The filled-in vaulted undercroft had its own (now-buried) floor some distance below the present floor level of the kitchen; but the vault rose at least a metre above that floor level, as the brick arch still evident in the outer face of the kitchen's west wall shows. What sort of floor did the substantial barrel-vault itself support? How we wish there were more evidence to indicate the floor levels in the building that housed the undercroft! There are other undercrofts in the parish which seem to be only partly subterranean, basements rather than cellars. The undercroft of St Andrew's Cottage would - at the time it was built - have been only a few steps down from the lower medieval ground level of Church Plain. A suggestive arrangement of three floors, albeit in timber, exists in the weaving workshop behind Norwich House. Was that paralleled in White Cottage?

The purpose of the undercroft remains shrouded in mystery. It is often said that raw wool was stored in undercrofts or cellars to keep it cool, but there is no physical evidence to link White Cottage with weaving before the mid twentieth century. Two postcards (one line-drawn, the other a black-and-white photo) then call it a weaver's cottage, probably because Mr and Mrs J R S Johnston ran Worstead Hand Loom Weavers there between 1949 and 1952. Another suggestion - from Edwin Rose - was that the undercroft was a cheese vault, but a cellar covered by a wooden floor would have been cool enough to store dairy products. A connection with the medieval market seems inescapable: the evidence of the brickwork supports the contention that the undercroft building was extended to form the L-shaped footprint of the second phase of the building's history, shown in red on the plan above. It is highly likely that only after the market's demise in 1666 did White Cottage become a dwelling.

In the second phase that belongs to the later seventeenth century the ingle-nook fireplace and chimney (2) were built against the north gable wall: the left hand return is built in bricks of that date but is not tied into the back wall of the ingle-nook. All or part of the barrel-vault seems to have been removed, as the broken brick-ends suggest (3). The south gable wall was built at the same time, but it was not tied into the front and back walls, suggesting that those walls (or parts of them) were built in timber with a wattle and daub infill or even in clay lump (a surviving example of clay lump building is the former chapel in Mill Lane beyond the Worstead parish boundary in Smallburgh). A close examination of the existing Flemish bond brickwork shows that the front and back walls have been altered and repaired many times.

Phase three of the building saw the first raising of the roof and the installation of an upper floor. The south gable wall evidences three rooflines: they can still be seen from the outside but were more visible when the plaster was removed from the small bedroom in 1999. The first roofline was that of the later seventeenth century, when it is likely that the main room of the cottage was open to the rafters. The date of the second roofline - a metre or so higher - is uncertain, but it must be some time before the cottage was divided (see below), because building work in 2004 revealed an opening at first floor level behind the chimney in the south gable wall, perhaps for a trapdoor or a window, which was blocked when the chimney was built in the later eighteenth century. The second roofline allowed the insertion of eaves windows in the brickwork of the east and west walls of the small bedroom, but the plaster was not removed in the larger bedroom. The upper floor may have been accessed by ladder via the 'coffin trap' that still exists to the left of the south chimney stack (6).

Fig 131 South gable interior view showing previous rooflines.

In phase four the building was divided into two cottages. On the south gable wall there now stands a second fireplace and chimney (6). In 1999 a cupboard crudely built of brick with a Georgian door stood to the right of the fireplace. Its removal revealed that the fireplace and chimney were not tied into the gable wall and had thus been added after the wall was built. A room of some twenty-one by twelve feet surely did not need a second fireplace. Further evidence for the division of the cottage was provided by the remains of a partition wall of reclaimed timber with a double skin of reed and daub (7) and by the window which filled the top half of what was once clearly a door-opening (8). The deeds also confirm the division of the cottage. In 1801 John Shalders was admitted by the manor court of Sloley with the Members to a copyhold tenement and land measuring nine feet by twenty-four: the smaller end of the present living room is nine feet wide. These measurements exclude the covered passageway with its curved front gable of probable eighteenth century date, which may have given access to the property behind owned by Sir George Berney Brograve in 1827. The partition of the cottage had occurred before 1801, but probably not long before. When the cottage reverted to a single dwelling is uncertain, but a map of 1827 associated with the enclosure shows that Jacob Shalders owned the whole property, which is not shown as divided. When the two cottages reverted to one, recycled timbers framed the opening made in the partition wall (7).

The fourth phase probably also saw the cottage roof raised to its present height, because the stud wall with a single skin of reed and daub which divides the two bedrooms extends to the third roofline and has not been altered, except for the insertion of a door when the two halves of the cottage were reunited. The present staircase rising out of the kitchen is a relatively modern insertion. In the larger of the two cottages the beam parallel to and near the back wall of the downstairs front room seems to have topped a partition behind which stairs rose to the upper storey. This suggestion is reinforced by changes to the pattern of the relatively wide floor boards (9-12 inches) above (10). After the partition was removed downstairs, a beam was also inserted across the middle of the ceiling below to support the rather flimsy beams of the upper floor: its wear and its fixings suggest it was once part of Norfolk's sea defences.

To this fourth phase probably belong the two small out-buildings and cobbled yards added to the building's western boundary: their footings were revealed when we took up an uneven part of the floor of what is now the dining room, which was added along with a bathroom in 1955. Two identical stores or coal sheds suggest one for each cottage. These were incorporated into a lean-to extension (9), outlined in blue on the plan above, probably in late Victorian or in Edwardian times, when such improvements in living arrangements were common. A further Victorian or Edwardian improvement was the insertion of a fireplace in the smaller bedroom. A sheet of metal was laid on the floorboards and the fireplace and its brick flue were built straight on the boards! The flue followed the curve of the chimney built for the fireplace below. The fireplace was blocked when we arrived: we found a George VI stamp among the rubbish left in it.

4. A possible timeline for White Cottage

In 1617 or before: phase 1 - the building containing the undercroft

1617: the date inscribed on the beam that became the bressumer

1666: the market moved to North Walsham

later 1600s: phase 2 - the undercroft building extended into the
L-shaped cottage
the ingle-nook and the north chimney built
the south gable wall built

early to mid 1700s: phase 3 - the first raising of the roof

before 1801: phase 4 - the division of the cottage into two
the second fireplace and chimney built
the roof raised to its present height

by 1827: the two dwellings reverted to one

the later 1800s or early 1900s: the fireplace added to the second bedroom

1949: the garden extended to 0.15 of an acre

1949-52: Johnstons' Hand Loom Weavers based in the cottage

1955: the flat-roof extension (bathroom & dining room) added

1999: restoration begun

5. White Cottage as part of the Shalders estate

The deeds cast some light on property owned by the Shalders family. In 1810 the court of the Manor of Sloley with the Members admitted Jacob Shalders (the Younger) to a tenement and land of 9 x 24 feet (the smaller end of the cottage). He and his successors were technically copyhold tenants. In the Middle Ages a copyholder was a serf who held land and other property from the manorial lord. Changes of tenancy were recorded in the manorial roll and a copy of the entry was given to the new tenant - for a fee! After the end of serfdom the copyholder became a tenant of the manorial lord. The copyhold on White Cottage was extinguished in 1935 and the tenure became freehold. Jacob's father John, who died in 1809, had held it since 1801 and John's father Jacob (the Elder) from 1787. A deed of covenant of 1861 relating to White Cottage shows that the Shalders family owned property across Worstead from at least as early as 1777. A map of 1827 identifies their properties in central Worstead as Norwich House, the Thatched House, a property to its rear at the end of the back lane behind Honing Row, part of Haggar House, most of Swann's Yard (then called Shalders' Yard) and all of White Cottage. Jacob (the Younger) ran his drapery and grocery in Norwich House.

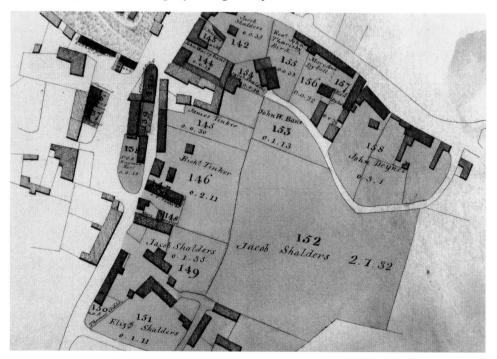

Fig 132 Detail of 1827 map - NRO ref C/Sca2/342

The deeds also tell us that Jacob Shalders mortgaged his freehold and copyhold property for £1200 to Sir Samuel Bignold in May 1835 or 1836 (two deeds conflict). Jacob had not repaid the £1200 by his death in 1857 and Sir Samuel claimed the property. The court of the Manor of Sloley with the Members admitted Sir Samuel to the copyhold of White Cottage in 1860, and the courts of other manors no doubt admitted him to Jacob's other copyholds. Sir Samuel mortgaged the whole estate but sold all the copyholds for £605 to Daniel Dyball of Wroxham. Was he related to the Dyball family who - the 1827 map shows - held the post office in Honing Row? The sale included White Cottage and its land, described as plot 137 on the enclosure map of 1827. A contemporary deed describes this plot as five perches (a standard perch was 5.5 yards): if this meant five perches square, then it included all the land on which White Cottage now stands from the front wall in the east to the far edge of the present concrete path in the west, and from the covered passageway in the south to Jean's Cottage in the north. Daniel Dyball died in June 1876. The complex provisions of his will were hard to disentangle. His son and chief heir Edward mortgaged the whole estate for £1000 in 1876 and for a further £200 in 1878, but Edward died intestate in August 1879. Disagreements in the Dyball family led to the Court of Chancery, which ordered the sale of part or all of the estate to satisfy the creditors. White Cottage, lot 7 in the auction of 1884, was bought for £65 by builder Robert Baldwin of Smallburgh.

6. Later owners of the cottage

	Purchase price
Robert Baldwin 1884-1912	£65
Robert Henry Baldwin (Robert's son) 1912-41	
Constance Baldwin (Robert Henry's widow) 1941-45	
Ellen Constance Drake (Constance's daughter) 1945-46	
Mabel Flowerday Hunn of Worstead Post Office 1946-49	£80
Arthur William Philpot 1949	£1260
John Robert Sherwin Johnston 1949-52	£850
Richard Youels Marples of Billingford 1952-59	£1000

Grace Marples (his mother) 1959-83   £1100

Richard & Betty Marples (Grace's son & daughter) 1983-99

Peter & Margaret Brice 1999-2014

Andrew & Wendy Millar 2014-

7. Some occupants of the cottage

James Grimes, village postman and shoemaker, was in occupation when Ellen Drake inherited the cottage in 1945. His tenancy was presumably arranged by the Baldwin family: James, nick-named 'Snob' or 'Snobby' as many shoemakers were, was listed as a shoemaker in Kelly's Directory of 1904 and oral testimony from a Mrs Lack puts her uncle James Grimes in the cottage in the 1920s and perhaps earlier. He made boots and shoes in a workshop in the back garden and sold them from his shop in the covered passageway (11) beside the cottage: pieces of leather and heel trims from boots and shoes were found in the shed, but the present well-worn bench is not full of the tacks to be expected in a cobbler's bench. Did James Grimes bury the shoe and quern stone under the kitchen floor? He left the cottage in December 1946, when Ellen Drake sold it.

Mr and Mrs J R S Johnston owned and occupied the cottage in 1949-52, working as hand loom weavers (see chapter 6). The cottage still holds their nameplate - Johnstons Hand Loom Weavers. Their letterhead pictures White Cottage, names its directors as J R S Johnston, J A Johnston and M E Gooch, and records its registered office as 35 Exchange Street, Norwich. A piece of their cloth, woven, it is said, in a shed on the top lawn, remains in the cottage.

8. THE FUTURE OF WORSTEAD'S PAST

Researching this book has been an exciting journey into Worstead's rich past, but this last chapter is about preserving the future of that past.

Fig 133 The Weaving Workshop behind Norwich House.

1. Delving deeper into Worstead's more distant past

The bald summary of Worstead's prehistory in Chapter 1 does less than justice to the archaeology of the parish. It is unlikely that professional archaeologists will be able to do a systematic survey of the parish, because most of their time is absorbed by rescue archaeology and by excavations required by the local authority's planning department. Such excavations are useful, as we have seen in relation to Worstead's market place (Chapter 2), but they are essentially random. However field-walking by a team of trained amateurs might tell us more about the parish before 1066 and about the extent of the medieval settlement when worsted was king.

The research that we have done so far indicates that there is more to be learned about the parish from national and local archives, for example from census records, parish registers, electoral registers, churchwarden's accounts, Parish Council minutes, and newspaper reports. For instance Worstead's last weaver, John Cubitt, came from a long line of Cubitts in Worstead: his surname was spelt as Kybyte at the time of the Great Revolt of 1381 (see Chapter 2). A survey of the parish registers between 1589 and 1764 yields twenty-nine Cubitt baptisms and ten Cubitt marriages, which cry out for further exploration. From 1841 the comparison of parish registers with census records offers a mine of information to those skilled in genealogical research. As each piece of new evidence is discovered, it prompts new questions and starts new searches. That is why no written history is ever the last word on any topic and why the study of history is endlessly fascinating.

2. Recording Worstead's recent past

Since World War II Worstead has seen many changes, becoming more residential and less commercial. All the shops have gone. The post office was run in the mid twentieth century by Mabel Hunn in the bow-fronted shop at the bottom of Church Plain, now called the Old Post Office. So the telephone kiosk of the type K6, designed by Sir Giles Gilbert Scott in 1935, was sited nearby in Front Street: it is now a listed building (NHER 47428). Worstead's last post office was located once more in Back Street with its door beside the present E II R post box. Run by Allison Henderson in the late twentieth and the early twenty-first century, it was the last shop in the parish. Such changes often go unrecorded because people think that they will remember them, but they rarely do so with any precision. When did Allison finally close the post office?

Worstead owes a great debt of gratitude to Ian Rendall and the team who wrote *Worstead Woven* (2000) for recording the memories of parishioners in the more recent past. Such recollections are very valuable, even if - as we know - every retelling of an event from memory inevitably involves some unconscious editing that subtly alters the story. So an urgent task waits to be done, the recording of the memories of the people who have always lived in Worstead, before those memories are lost as they so often are. Paul Staples' recollections of his mother Margaret - Worstead's first qualified district nurse from 1936 - show that the memories are still there, waiting to be collected. And Gavin Paterson's recollections of farming in Worstead are - at the time of writing - being recorded in print, under the provisional title of *Breeding Success*, a reference to his prize dairy herd of Holstein Friesian cattle.

Fig 134 & 135 Front Cover – now out of print.   *The first Festival programme*

In the programme of the first Worstead Festival in 1966 the Vicar wrote: *'We hope that this Festival will not be the last, but the first of a series. We very much want to add such things as playing fields and a community centre to the amenities of Worstead.'* The village now has both, thanks to the continued success of the Festival. The Queen Elizabeth Hall is a remarkable facility for the parish. Even here there is history: how many of the more recent incomers to the parish realise that the opening of the Hall by Queen Elizabeth the Queen Mother in 1985 caused steps (*Fig 119*) from the former Worstead House to be relocated in the south-west corner of the churchyard, so that she could walk from the Hall to St Mary's? The Festival has also contributed to many worthy causes in and around the parish and has shown what great things can be achieved by a small community working harmoniously together. The story of the Festival is best told by those who created it and by those who have sustained it over many years. As I write there are plans afoot to celebrate the first fifty years of the Festival in July 2015.

3. Conserving Worstead's architectural heritage

The grander buildings of Worstead appear on the Heritage Trail maps and leaflets and in the Norfolk Heritage Environment Record. The value of the parish's architecture is recognised by its many entries on the National Heritage List for England. The roll begins with the Church of St Mary the Virgin, listed grade I, and the undercroft of St Andrew's Cottage, listed grade II*. Listed grade II are

Bengate Farm House
Church Cottage
Geoffrey the Dyer House
Gothic Lodge
Lacey Farm
The Manor House and its wall
The New Inn (now the White Lady)
Norwich House and its weaver's workshop
Swan Cottage
The Thatched House,
New Lane Cottage
Worstead Hall Farmhouse,
Worstead Hall Stables
Worstead Mill
K6 telephone box
The Baptist Chapel, Meeting Hill
Stone Cross by Tollgate Farm

All these buildings would benefit from further research, but there are also many fine and interesting buildings that have escaped the attention of English Heritage, because local knowledge is often not sought by such national groups. However the draft Conservation Area Appraisal of 2008 (see below) included many but not all of the buildings mentioned in the text:

The Primitive Methodist Chapel,
St Andrew's Cottage
The Old Post Office
Haggar House
Laburnum Cottage
Benefield House
Laurels Farmhouse

Laurels Farm Barns
Clemsea House
White Cottage
Church View House (the former King's Head),
Manor Farm Barns
Holly Grove House
Lyngate House
No. 6 Honing Row
Weaver's Cottage and the other Baptist buildings in Meeting Hill
The Old White Horse in Briggate.

There are other properties that might have been included. For instance, I am grateful to Eve Wilson for details relating to 1 Watson's Yard. The cottage within the Yard probably belongs to the mid eighteenth century, while the extension with the bow-fronted window dates from the early to mid nineteenth century. The chimney and its gable wall shows the house and its extension were once thatched. The extension housed the pork butcher's shop of Mrs Sarah Watson in 1883 and in 1902, but she was no longer trading in 1904. Even quite recent buildings have their part to play in Worstead's history: their sites may have a longer history that will bear further exploration.

Fig 136 Roofs of Watson's Yard

The built environment of the parish also reveals a wealth of architectural details. Before the arrival of pantiles in the seventeenth century, most Worstead roofs were thatched and thus needed a steep pitch. Many of these steep-pitched roofs have since been raised to accommodate a second storey under a roof of lower pitch, while retaining the same ridge height. One good example, among quite a number across the parish, is the west end gable of The Retreat in Honing Row. Sometimes an original lower-pitched roof is later raised and with it the ridge height: this happened twice at White Cottage in Front Street. More rarely a steep-pitched roof and its ridge height are lowered, most clearly at 1 Watson's Yard. Alongside these changes in rooflines are examples of Dutch gables, popular in the late seventeenth and early eighteenth century: most prominent are the gables of the Thatched House on Church Plain.

Fig 137 Watson's Yard

Fig 138 The Thatched House

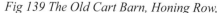

Fig 139 The Old Cart Barn, Honing Row,

Fig 140 Plinth at The White Lady

The walls of buildings and their boundaries hold much interest. We have referred before to the medieval limestone taken from the rebuilding of St Mary's or the demolition of St Andrew's. Many pieces, some showing Gothic mouldings, were reused rather erratically in post-medieval secular buildings, most obviously in Norwich House and Bengate Farm. At times pieces of limestone are found close to the foundation of a wall, as in the cottages in Sloley Road opposite Laurels Farm Barn before its conversion to dwellings.

Fig 141 Sloley Road cottages opposite Laurels Farm Barn

There are also many differing patterns in the use of brick and flint. Chapter 2 has drawn attention to the flushwork of St Mary's, but there is a plinth of squared flint flushwork on the front of the New Inn (now the White Lady): did the flint come from one of the churches, or was it specially knapped? Numerous buildings across the parish have halved flint as the facing of their front walls. Chapter 3 has mentioned diapering, the diamond decoration outlined in contrasting brick or flint quite common in the sixteenth and early seventeenth century: diapering appears in black header brick diamonds in the red brick west wall of Geoffrey the Dyer House in School Road; and in red brick in the flint walling of the cottages opposite Laurels Farm Barn. Chapter 3 has also noted the decorative platbands or mouldings which separate the storeys of the Manor House, the Thatched House and St Andrew's Cottage. Another fine plaitband is to be seen at the Old White Horse in Briggate and one was recorded in Starling's drawing of the stylish house that once stood on the west side of Church Plain facing Norwich House. Most belong to the later seventeenth or early eighteenth century, but there are later variations on the same theme, as - for instance - on the house between the Old White Horse and the bridge in Briggate.

Fig 142-4 Platband details in Church Plain

Three undercrofts have been mentioned in various chapters above, those beneath St Andrews Cottage, in the weaving workshop behind Norwich House, and under White Cottage in Front Street. There may have been others across the parish, but as the ground level has risen over time, undercrofts may have become less accessible from outside and more damp. Some may have turned into cellars, like those of the New Inn, mentioned in Chapter 4. The arch almost at ground level in the front of Geoffrey the Dyer House is probably that of a cellar window: it can hardly be an external entrance so close to the road.

We may think that historians and archaeologists will have recorded everything of real significance, but that is not so. Laurie Ashton brought the helmeted effigy outside St Mary's (discussed in Chapter 2) to the notice of the team designing the Heritage Trails in 2012, and only then was it entered in the Norfolk Historic Environment Record (NHER 58019). Thanks to Laurie's persistence the effigy was preserved during building works at the church early in 2015 and as I write efforts are being made to afford it greater protection. The building works revealed that the effigy had been cemented in place as the lid of a soak-away, quite possibly when the church roof was restored in 1899-1900. This raises new questions: for instance, where was it sited in the centuries before it became the cover of the soak-away, inside St Mary's, St Andrew's or perhaps elsewhere? Laurie's good work shows that there are always new things to be discovered and there is great pleasure to be had in the hunt. The story of the effigy also indicates that the visible features noted above in Worstead's architecture should be recorded: the altered rooflines and Dutch gables; the reused ecclesiastical limestone; the flint flushwork and other knapped flint in secular buildings; the diapering and the platbands; and the undercrofts and cellars. What might we learn, what connections might we make, if such features were catalogued and mapped?

Fig 145 The Effigy and soakaway exposed in 2015. Courtesy The Whitworth Co-Partnership LLP

There is also more research to be done on the documentary evidence for individual properties, because even seemingly dull documents contained within a house's deeds are often informative. A deed of enfranchisement of 26 September 1924, brought to my notice by Laurie Ashton, is headed *Norwich Chapter Estates, Worstead St Andrew Manor, the Ecclesiastical Commissioners for England to Mr Samuel Grimes, Baker.* The Manor of Worstead St Andrew had by then passed into the possession of the Ecclesiastical Commissioners, but the deed does not say when. The deed releases Samuel Grimes from the copyhold tenure by which St Andrew's Cottage was held of the Manor of Worstead St Andrew, so that he can now hold it freehold. The plot is defined as number 144 on the Enclosure Map of 1827, when it was bounded by the properties of Jacob Shalders, John Wacey Beane, and Sir George Berney Brograve. Add this to the rest of the deeds of St Andrew's Cottage and to those of the neighbouring properties, and what a lot of history might be revealed. Now that house deeds are no longer needed to establish one's legal title to a property at the Land Registry, they become more vulnerable, no longer held securely by a solicitor or bank. However they also become more available as a resource for historical research, for which they need to be preserved, preferably in the Norfolk Record Office.

Fig 146 Church Cottage detail viewed from the cemetery.

Worstead is fortunate that most of the owners of its historic buildings take their responsibilities seriously, but buildings do deteriorate. One that is suffering is the Obelisk (*31* - NHER 7582). This strange building is sited just beyond the parish boundary but is part of Worstead's history, if we believe the often-quoted story that Elizabeth Berney built this tower of rendered brick and flint topped by a glass and cast iron gazebo, so that she could through her telescope, keep a jealous eye on her elder sister Julian in Worstead. The ruins of Briggate Mill became so dangerous that the District Council had most of it demolished in 2012, but how well was it recorded beforehand? Two small losses without the benefit of recording point to a more insidious process: the brick and flint forge behind Forge Cottage was allowed to deteriorate to the point that it reputedly fell down; and the village pound for stray animals at the north end of Laurels Farm Barn was lost in the conversion of the barn into two good houses, perhaps because visibility round the sharp bend was deemed more important. Do the gains outweigh the losses? Such questions need to be asked with persistence. Worstead's history imposes tasks on us and our representatives on the Parish, District and County Councils:

1. to secure the preservation of historic buildings of both national and local significance;
2. to ensure that the historic grain of the parish is respected in new development, which should be justified by a heritage assessment;
3. to ensure that the design and the materials chosen for new buildings complement those traditionally used in the parish and follow the historic building lines, such as those of Back Street, Front Street, Honing Row, and Meeting Hill.

Conservation areas are designed to help with these tasks, but their importance has been downgraded as reduced resources have changed political priorities. Worstead's Conservation Area was designated in 1973 and the uniqueness of Meeting Hill's Baptist settlement was acknowledged when it became a Conservation Area in 2001. The Worstead Conservation Area formed part of the North Norfolk Local Plan of 1998, when a Development Area was also established, including most of the village centre. The Development Area ceased to exist in North Norfolk's Local Development Framework Core Strategy of 2007-08. Then Worstead was classified as part of the countryside where development was restricted. In 2008 the District Council prepared a report *Worstead Conservation Area: Character Appraisal and Management Proposals.* This document had significant merits, although the Worstead Amenity Society wanted to propose amendments, but sadly conservation area appraisals are no longer part of best conservation practice: local vigilance thus becomes the best defence of our historic environment. In the early 2000s the District Council's Conservation Architect assured the Amenity Society that the Conservation Area would protect Worstead's historic environment. However, as early as 2008 a Planning Inspector, hearing a planning appeal in Honing Row, said that a tour of the village centre led her to conclude that some of its modern developments should never have been permitted!

Fig 147 Diapering to the rear wing of Geoffrey the Dyer House.

4. Footprints on the sands of time

This book has recorded many of the footprints that Worstead people have left on the sands of time. New footprints are being made all the time, but they are fragile. We need to preserve as many of them as possible, so that future historians will have the fullest evidence from which to write their studies of Worstead.

> *The lives of great men all remind us*
> *We can make our lives sublime,*
> *And, departing, leave behind us*
> *Footprints on the sands of time.*

Henry Wadsworth Longfellow (1807-92)

Fig 148 19ᵗʰ Century graffiti in the ringing chamber of St Mary's.

LIST OF ILLUSTRATIONS

Unless otherwise stated photographs and illustrations by Stefan Ganther

BIBLIOGRAPHY

Richard Allington-Smith *Henry Despenser, the Fighting Bishop*
Larks Press 2003

Anon *Struggles in Worstead*
Wesley Historical Society East Anglia District Magazine 114 summer 2009

T Ashwin & A Davison (Eds) *An Historical Atlas of Norfolk*
Phillimore 2005, third edition

Brian Ayers *Norwich, a Fine City*
Tempus 2003, second edition

J Barker *England Arise: the People, the King and the Great Revolt of 1381*
Little, Brown 2014

J C Barringer (Ed) *Faden's Map of Norfolk*
Larks Press 1989

C Barringer *Exploring the Norfolk Village*
Poppyland Publishing 2005

C Barringer *Exploring the Norfolk Market Town*
Poppyland Publishing 2011

Neil Batcock *The Ruined and Disused Churches of Norfolk*
East Anglian Archaeology report 51, 1991

Mark Bell *Freedom to Form: Baptist movements in the English Revolution* in
C Durston & J Maltby *Religion in Revolutionary England*
Manchester UP 2006

H S Bennett *The Pastons and their England*
CUP 1922 &1968

Francis Blomefield *History of Norfolk*
reprinted in eleven volumes in 1805-10

J Boyes & R Russell *The Canals of Eastern England*
David & Charles 1977

C A Bradbury *A Norfolk Saint for a Norfolk Man: William of Norwich and Sir James Hobart at Holy Trinity Church in Loddon*
Norfolk Archaeology XLVI part IV 2013

P Brooks *Norfolk Miscellany*
Breedon Books 2009

Bruce M S Campbell *The Extent and Layout of Commonfields in Eastern Norfolk*
Norfolk Archaeology XXXVIII part I 1981

A Carter & S Wade Martins (Eds) *A Year in the Field*
Centre for East Anglian Studies 1987

P Cattermole & S Cotton *Medieval Parish Church Building in Norfolk*
Norfolk Archaeology XXXVIII part III 1983

Barbara Cornford *Medieval Flegg 1086-1500*
Larks Press 2002

S Cotton *Medieval Roodscreens in Norfolk*
Norfolk Archaeology XL part I 1987

A S Culley *A Manual of the Baptist Church at Worstead*
printed in Norwich 1898

J Davies *The Land of Boudica*
Oxbow Books 2008

BIBLIOGRAPHY

N Davis (Ed) *The Paston Letters*
Oxford 1983

Daniel Defoe *Tour through the Eastern Counties 1724*
Eastern Counties Magazine Ltd 1984

D Dymond *The Norfolk Landscape*
Hodder & Stoughton 1985

J Ede & N Virgoe (Eds) *The 1851 Census of Religious Worship for Norfolk*
Norfolk Record Society 1998

J Ede, N Virgoe & T Williamson *Halls of Zion: Chapels and Meeting-Houses of Norfolk*
Centre for East Anglian Studies 1994

C Forder *A History of the Paston School*
published by the Governors 1975

S Hart *Flint Architecture of East Anglia*
Giles de la Mare Publishers 2000

N Heard *Wool: East Anglia's Golden Fleece*
Terence Dalton 1970

R Hilton *Bondmen Made Free: Medieval Peasant Movements and the English Rising of 1381*
Methuen 1973

Alice Hogge *God's Secret Agents*
HarperCollins 2005

R A Houlbrooke (Ed) *The Letter Book of John Parkhurst*
Norfolk Record Society 1974 & 1975

C B Jewson *St Mary's, Norwich*
reprinted from the Baptist Quarterly 1941

C B Jewson *The Baptists in Norfolk*
The Carey Kingsgate Press 1957

C B Jewson *The Return of Conventicles in Norwich Diocese 1669*
Norfolk Archaeology XXXIII part I 1962

R Lee *Unquiet Country: Voices of the Rural Poor 1820-1880*
Windgather 2005

M D Jennings *Royal Air Force Coltishall: Fighter Station*
Old Forge Publishing 2007

A Longcroft & S Wade-Martins (Eds) *Building an Education: An Historical and Architectural Study of Rural Schools and Schooling in Norfolk c.1800-1944*
Journal of the Norfolk Historic Buildings Group volume 5 2013

E Martin & M Satchell '*Wheare most Inclosures be*'
East Anglian Archaeology report 124, 2008

R Malster *The Norfolk and Suffolk Broads*
Phillimore 2003

R Malster *Maritime Norfolk*
Poppyland Publishing 2012

S Margeson, B Ayers & Heywood (Eds) *A Festival of Norfolk Archaeology*
Norfolk & Norwich Archaeological Society 1996

R Matthew *Robert Toppes, Medieval Mercer of Norwich*
Norfolk and Norwich Heritage Trust 2013

F Meeres *Norfolk in the First World War*
Phillimore 2004

F Meeres *Norfolk in the Second World War*
Phillimore 2006

G A Metters (Ed) *The Parliamentary Survey of Dean and Chapter Properties in and around Norwich in 1649*
Norfolk Record Society 1985

BIBLIOGRAPHY

T Morris '*Made in Norwich*' - *700 Years of Textile History*
Published by Nick Williams 2008

M Partridge *Farm Tools through the Ages*
Osprey 1973

T Pestell *Landscapes of Monastic Foundation: the Establishment*
of Religious Houses in East Anglia c.650-1200
Boydell 2004

N Pevsner & Bill Wilson *The Buildings of England: Norfolk 1*
Penguin 1997, second edition

Phyllis E Pobst *The Register of William Bateman, Bishop of Norwich, 1344-55*
Boydell Press 1996

Ursula Priestley *The Fabric of Stuffs: the Norwich textile industry from 1365*
Centre for East Anglian Studies 1990

C Rawcliffe & R Wilson (Eds) *Medieval Norwich* and *Norwich Since 1550*
both Hambledon 2004

I Rendall et al. *Worstead Woven*
Worstead Festival & Parish Council 2000

Matthew Rice *Building Norfolk*
Frances Lincoln Ltd 2008

Bruce Robinson & Edwin J Rose *Norfolk Origins: Roads and Tracks*
Poppyland Publishing 2008

K I Sandred *The Place-names of Norfolk, Part 2*
English Placename Society 1996

H W Saunders *An Introduction to the Rolls of Norwich Cathedral Priory*
Jarrold 1930

J R Shinners Jr. *The Veneration of Saints at Norwich Cathedral in the Fourteenth Century*
Norfolk Archaeology XL part II, 1988

P Slavin *Bread and Ale for the Brethren: the provisioning of Norwich Cathedral Priory*
University of Hertfordshire Press 2012

S Smith *And They Loved Not Their Lives Unto Death*
Menin House 2012

A F Sutton *The Early Linen and Worsted Industry of Norfolk and the Evolution of the London Mercers' Company*
Norfolk Archaeology XL part III, 1989

T H Swales *The Redistribution of the Monastic Land in Norfolk at the Dissolution*
Norfolk Archaeology XXXIV part I, 1966

M & W Vaughan-Lewis *Aylsham Old Hall at Old Market*
Norfolk Archaeology XLVI part IV, 2013

S Wade Martins *Changing Agriculture in Georgian and Victorian Norfolk*
Poppyland Publishing 2002

H B Walters *Inventories of Norfolk Church Goods (1552): Hundred of Tunstead*
Norfolk Archaeology XXXIII part IV 1965

Tom Williamson *The Origins of Norfolk*
Manchester UP 1993

Tom Williamson *England's Landscape: East Anglia*
HarperCollins 2006

Tom Williamson & A Macnair *William Faden and Norfolk's 18th Century Landscape*
Windgather 2010

BIBLIOGRAPHY

W W Williamson *Saints on Norfolk Rood-Screens and Pulpits*
Norfolk Archaeology XXXI part III 1987

D Yaxley *A Researcher's Glossary*
The Larks Press 2003